MONUMENTAL REMAINS
OF THE
DUTCH EAST INDIA COMPANY
IN THE
PRESIDENCY OF MADRAS

ARCHAEOLOGICAL SURVEY OF INDIA
NEW IMPERIAL SERIES VOLUME XXV

MONUMENTAL REMAINS OF THE DUTCH EAST INDIA COMPANY IN THE PRESIDENCY OF MADRAS

ALEXR. REA

GYAN

Published by

GYAN

Gyan Publishing House
5, Ansari Road
Daryaganj, New Delhi-110002
Phone: 011-47034999, 9811692060
E-mail: books@gyanbooks.com

Distribution Network
gyanbooks.com
India, USA, Canada, UK, Australia, France

ISBN : 978-81-212-3787-1 (PB)
First Published, Madras, 1897

2nd Impression 2020

Printed at: Gyan Press, Delhi.

ARCHÆOLOGICAL SURVEY OF INDIA.

NEW IMPERIAL SERIES, VOLUME XXV.

MONUMENTAL REMAINS

OF THE

DUTCH EAST INDIA COMPANY

IN THE

PRESIDENCY OF MADRAS.

BY

ALEXR. REA,

SUPERINTENDENT, ARCHÆOLOGICAL SURVEY, MADRAS; MEMBER OF THE ROYAL ASIATIC SOCIETY OF GREAT BRITAIN AND IRELAND.

MADRAS:

PRINTED AND PUBLISHED BY THE SUPERINTENDENT, GOVERNMENT PRESS.

CALCUTTA—THACKER, SPINK & CO. BOMBAY—THACKER & CO., LD.

LONDON—TRUBNER & CO. AND W. H. ALLEN & CO.

LEIPZIG—OTTO HARRASSOWITZ.

1897.

REFERENCES.

Standing Information regarding the Administration of the Madras Presidency, 1879.
Manual of the Chingleput District, Madras, 1879.
Manual of the Ganjám District, Madras, 1882.
Government Order; Proceedings of the Madras Government.
A Descriptive and Historical Account of the Gódávari District, Madras, 1878.
India, by Wm. Robertson, D.D., F.R.S., Principal of the University of Edinburgh, 1791 and 1827.
Journal of the Asiatic Society of Bengal.
Manual of the Kistna District, Madras, 1883.
List of Antiquarian Remains in the Presidency of Madras, Vol. I, 1882.
The Madura Country, Madras, 1868.
Madras Manual of the Administration, Vol. I, 1885.
Madras Journal of Literature and Science.
Government Central Museum, Madras Coin Catalogue, 1888.
Malabar, Madras. Two volumes, 1887.
A Collection of Treaties, &c., Malabar, Madras, 1891.
Manual of the Nellore District, Madras, 1873.
Manual of the South Arcot District, Madras, 1878.
Elements of South Indian Palæography, 1878.
Manual of the Tanjore District, Madras, 1883.
Manual of the Tinnevelly District, Madras, 1879.
Manual of the Trichinopoly District, Madras, 1878.
Records of the Madras Government Secretariat.

CONTENTS.

PART I.—HISTORICAL MEMOIR.

PART II.—MONUMENTAL REMAINS.

PART III.—INDO-DUTCH COINAGE.

LIST OF PLATES.

LIST OF PLATES.

REPORT

OF

THE ARCHÆOLOGICAL SURVEY OF SOUTHERN INDIA.

MONUMENTAL REMAINS OF THE DUTCH EAST INDIA COMPANY.

PART I.—HISTORICAL MEMOIR.

CHAPTER I.

SIXTEENTH CENTURY.

THE chief among the European nations, who, on the revival of the commercial spirit, acquired a large share of the early trade with India, were the Venetians. During the fifteenth century they had almost a complete monopoly, and their merchants made enormous profits.[1] They do not seem to have had many, if any, actual settlements in India; nor did they, in conducting the bulk of the trade, even have any direct communication with that continent.[2] (The remains of a traditional European colony of A.D. 1224, exist on the coast, near Pedda Ganjám in the Kistna district. It is supposed to have been either Genoese or Venetian. It is known as Faringidibba.[3]) Their commerce was carried on through Oriental intermediaries, from whom they received the products of the country, and carried and sold these in the European markets.

The goods were carried overland by caravan, and the numerous transhipments and passage through dangerous countries added greatly to their value when they reached Europe. Those of small bulk and high value, such as cloves, nutmegs, mace, gems, pearls and the like, were conveyed from the Persian Gulf up the Tigris to Bassora and Bagdad, and thence to some Mediterranean port. Articles of bulk, such as pepper, ginger, cinnamon, and a portion of the valuable articles, went by the ancient route of the Red Sea and across the desert to Alexandria.[4]

One of the events, which directly contributed to the destruction of Venetian commerce with the East, was the discovery by the Portuguese, in 1498, of the direct route to India by the Cape of Good Hope. In spite of great opposition, it rapidly supplanted the ancient desert roadway, and became that by which the various European companies, who were to follow, pursued their trade.

The Portuguese, at first led by a series of selected officers, and supported by their kings—who considered the encouragement of the eastern trade a chief object of

---

[1] *Ind.*, p. 127. [2] *Ib.* [3] *Lists of Antiq.*, p. 82. [4] *Ind.*, p. 115.

Government—rapidly extended their possessions in the East and secured the monopoly of the commerce of India.[5] "In every part of the East they were received with respect, in which they had acquired the absolute command; they carried on trade then without rival or controul; they prescribed to the natives the terms of their mutual intercourse; they often set what price they pleased on goods which they purchased; and were thus enabled to import from Indostan and the regions beyond it, whatever is useful, rare or agreeable, in greater abundance, and of more various kinds than had been known formerly in Europe."[6] The accumulated expenses of the numerous transhipments of the overland route, rendered unnecessary by the direct voyage round the Cape of Good Hope, enabled the Portuguese to sell their goods at a much cheaper rate and among classes of the community than before had been possible. Notwithstanding its lucrative returns, the trade remained in their hands undisputed and without a rival for about a century. They were the first Europeans to form regular trading settlements in India. When they first visited the countries of Asia—to whence their trade extended—from the Malabar coasts to the China seas, they found them inhabited by peoples highly civilized, accustomed to intercourse with strangers, and well conversant with the advantages of commerce. In the early period of European commercial relations with the East, trade "was a simple mercantile transaction, confined to the purchase either of the material productions of the country, such as spices, precious stones, pearls, &c., or of the manufactures which abounded among an industrious race of men, such as silk and cotton stuffs, porcelane, &c. Nothing more was requisite in conducting this trade than to settle a few skilful agents in proper places to prepare a proper assortment of goods for completing the cargoes of ships as soon as they arrived from Europe, or at the utmost to acquire the command of a few fortified stations, which might secure them admission into ports where they might careen in safety and find protection from the insults of any hostile power. There was no necessity of making any attempt to establish colonies, either for the cultivation of the soil or the conduct of manufactures. Both these remained, as formerly, in the hands of the natives."[7] This was the method followed by the early pioneers: the description has not equal application to the procedure of the later European adventurers.

"In no part of the earth do the natives depend so little upon foreign countries either for the necessaries or luxuries of life," therefore in all ages, gold and silver, particularly the latter, have been the commodities exported with the greatest profit to India. But, "if Europe had not been supplied with the gold and silver which it was necessary to carry to the markets of the East from sources richer and more abundant than her own impoverished mines, she must either have abandoned the trade with India altogether, or have continued it with manifest disadvantage." But "America opened her mines and poured in treasures upon Europe, ... and from that time to the present (1791) the English and Dutch have purchased the productions of China and Indostan with silver brought from the mines of Mexico and Peru."[8]

Towards the end of the sixteenth century, a series of events occurred, which first threatened the Portuguese monopoly, and afterwards led to its complete overthrow. On the death of Henry I. and the subjugation of Portugal by Spain, the prestige of the former received a severe blow. The control of its eastern trading settlements passed into the hands of the latter. In 1580–81 Holland declared its independence of Spain. Incensed at this, and wishing to humble the Portuguese, Spain debarred the Amsterdam

[5] *Ind.*, p. 136. [6] *Ibid.* [7] *Ind.*, p. 167. [8] *Ind.*, p. 162.

merchants from trading with Lisbon. The seven United Provinces of the low countries had been but recently formed into a state, and were as yet without power or political influence. This restriction prevented the Dutch—whose subsistence depended almost solely on the carrying trade—from receiving their share of eastern produce, then only imported by the exclusive traders to the East, the Portuguese. They were thus obliged to direct their efforts in other directions. They settled on the Pomeroom and Essequibo rivers in Guiana in 1580.[9] In 1588 the naval power of Spain collapsed by the loss of the Armada, and the Antwerp merchants, who had gone to Amsterdam, thought they saw an opportunity for establishing a direct commerce with India. They had no longer to dread the superior naval power of those with whom they were destined to come into competition. At that time, a Papal license to trade with infidels was considered necessary. A bull had been granted in 1454 by Nicholas V. to Prince Henry of Portugal, authorizing him to trade with Muhammadans, and in 1502 another was issued to the same power, under which the King of Portugal was designated 'Lord of the Navigation Conquests, and Trade of Ethiopia, Arabia, Persia and India.'

The Dutch endeavoured to avoid interference with the rights thus sanctioned to Portugal, and, following the example of England, attempted to reach the East by sailing round the north coasts of Europe and Asia.[10]

Several attempts were made in this direction by William Barents in the years 1594, 1595 and 1596.

Failing to attain their object by this route, they were faced with the alternative of abandoning further efforts, or forcing themselves into competition with the monopolists: they chose the latter. The Portuguese would seem to have, to a certain extent, kept secret the particulars of their passage by the Cape of Good Hope; and to the Dutch Navigator Cornelius Houtman belongs the honour, not only of learning what the route was, but of being the first of his countrymen to follow it out. The Spanish had imprisoned him at Lisbon; and while there, he obtained from the Portuguese some information regarding their voyage round the Cape. On escaping to Amsterdam he prevailed on some of the chief merchants to send him in command of a mercantile expeditionary fleet of four vessels, which left the Texel on June 1st, 1595. He reached Sumatra in seventeen months, and finally came to Bantam in Java, where the Portuguese had a factory. Here the adventurers were ill-treated and imprisoned; but finally escaping, three ships returned to Holland in August 1598. They were honourably welcomed, and the success of the enterprise seeming assured, another fleet of eight ships was shortly got ready and sent out. Four of these returned in fifteen months with rich cargoes. During the course of the second expedition sent out under Houtman, the commander himself was killed.

In 1597 two Dutch ships succeeded in reaching India, but one was destroyed by six Portuguese vessels off Malacca, and the other was wrecked off the coast of Pegu.[11]

After the despatch of Houtman's expedition, another left under command of James Van Neck. He succeeded in reaching Amboyna and establishing trade. The Dutch also settled at Baroda.[12]

The Mauritius was first discovered by the Portuguese in 1505. It was taken by the Dutch in 1598, who named it after their Stadtholder, Prince Maurice of Nassau.[13]

---

[9] *Mad. Manl. Admn.*, p. 504.

[10] *Ind.*, pp. 161, 300; *Malbr. Manl.*, pp. 340; *Mad. Man. Admn.* p. 2.

[11] *Malbr. Manl.*, p. 336; *Mad. Manl. Admn.*, pp. 2, 156; *Tnvlly. Dt. Manl.*, pp. 45, 47.

[12] *Mad. Manl. Admn.*, p. 2; *Malbr. Manl.*, p. 336.

[13] *Mad. Manl. Admn.*, p. 2.

But for the ill-advised attempt of Spain to exclude them from even the secondary part they played in the transport of eastern commodities, it is possible that the Dutch might never have appeared in the East, and that they would have contented themselves with such a share as had before been allowed them. But by a strange turn of events, they were driven by the Portuguese themselves, or by those under whose protection the latter were, to contest the existing monopoly of trade, to ultimately drive out and completely supplant the monopolists.

CHAPTER II.

SEVENTEENTH CENTURY.

HAVING successfully overcome the obstacles planned to prevent their reaching the East, they had yet to secure a footing when there. The opposition of the Portuguese was still bitterly used in attempts to thwart them.

After the success of the enterprise had been demonstrated by the early voyagers, the dormant commercial spirit was roused, and independent companies were formed all over the United Provinces. Such measure of success as had yet been achieved was solely due to individual enterprise. But, foreseeing the greater results which could be obtained by combination, not only in securing a share of the trade, but in holding their own against the persecutions of the Portuguese, the funds of the various rival companies which had sprung up in Holland were incorporated, and the Dutch East India Company was formally instituted in 1602. Exclusive privileges of trading with the East were granted by the States-General to the Directors of the Company, and it gradually increased and secured the whole trade of the Spice Islands. It soon became a formidable factor in the power of the state.[14]

The Portuguese appeared first in Ceylon in 1505. In 1517 they came with a fleet, built a fort in Colombo, and forced the king to become a vassal of theirs, paying to them an annual tribute of cinnamon, rubies, sapphires and elephants. The first Dutch expedition arrived in 1602 and negociated an alliance with the King of Kandy.[15]

The rise of the new power had raised the apprehensions of the Spanish, and they did their utmost to check or defeat the encroachments of the Dutch on their monopoly. Unfortunately for them, they were without the necessary naval power to crush their rivals at sea; and they endeavoured to gain by underhand means what they could not accomplish by force. Representations were made at the courts of eastern potentates, with whom trading was ordinarily conducted, that the adventurers who had appeared on the scene were pirates.

The Dutch Admiral Heemskirk had, in the meantime, captured a richly laden Portuguese vessel on her way to Macao; and, having treated the prisoners with great generosity, received a letter of thanks from the chief Spanish authorities in the East. As a refutation of their attempts at detraction, he produced the letter at every port at which he called.[16]

The opposition the Dutch were encountering, caused them to turn on their rivals and attempt to dislodge them from the places where they had settled.

---

[14] *Mad. Manl. Admn.*, p. 159; *God. Dt. Manl.*, p. 195.
[15] *Mad. Manl. Admn.*, p. 118; *Tnvlly. Dt. Manl.*, pp. 45, 47.
[16] *Mad. Manl. Admn.*, p. 2.

Though they did, indeed, form new trading stations, it was principally after they had wrested from the Portuguese the settlements they had already formed.

Henceforward the progress of their rise was marked by a corresponding decline in the operations of their opponents.

Though at first clouded by occasional failures, the conflicts which mark subsequent relations between the two powers were generally to the Dutch; the Portuguese power waned, and they gradually disappeared from the scene. The Dutch, when they had secured it, in turn, became as aggressive in their monopoly as had been the power they had displaced and the Venetians before them. This exclusiveness was again, in turn, one of the factors which led to their subsequent overthrow.

In 1603 the Dutch, with a large European force, made an unsuccessful attempt to dislodge the Portuguese from Mozambique and Goa. In 1604 the Spaniards captured the Dutch settlements in the Indian Archipelago; but the occupation was of short duration.

In 1604–5 they had factories on the Malabar and Coromandel Coasts, in Ceylon, and in Java, at Jacotra and Bantam.[17]

A power which followed the Dutch, after the latter had prepared the way, was developed from the formation of a Company of London East India Merchants in 1599. Trading in the footsteps of the Dutch, they first tried their fortunes in the Spice Islands. There the two came in contact, and the bad feeling—which subsequently became so marked in all their transactions—was first developed.[18]

Some ships, sent out under Middleton in 1604, proceeded to Bantam and extended their trade to Banda and Amboyna. The Dutch at first received them well, but jealousies between them afterwards broke out. A contemporary of Middleton's, who afterwards succeeded him, in a voyage to Japan had a similar experience.[19]

In 1607 the Dutch had factories at Mocha, Cambay, Malabar, Ceylon, Coromandel, Bengal, Arakan, Pegu, Sumatra, Java, Camboja, Siam, Cochin China, Tonquin China and Japan. In addition were those taken from the Portuguese in the Moluccas and the Banda Islands.[20]

Hitherto the Dutch Trading Company had been as interlopers in the estimation of the Spaniards; but the extension of their operations could be no longer overlooked; and, in 1609, the rights of Holland to trade with India were formally recognized by the latter power.[21]

In 1609 [22] the Company founded a settlement at Pulicat, a seaport in the Chingleput district, 25 miles north of Madras. They built a fort—the ruins of which still exist—and named it 'Castel Geldria.' [23]

Ludovico di Varthema, the Bolognese, who travelled in the East from 1503 to 1508, visited many of the Portuguese possessions on the east and west coasts of India. One of these was Paleakate (Pulicat), described as 'a place of immense trade.' [24] It was then the chief port of trade with the Straits.[25] As this was fully a century before the Dutch occupation, it is probable that the Portuguese preceded them; or the trade referred to may have been solely in the hands of the natives.

---

[17] *Mad. Manl. Admn.*, p. 2.
[18] *Chingpt. Dt. Manl.*, p. 142.
[19] *Mad. Manl. Admn.*, p. 156.
[20] *Mad. Manl. Admn.*, p. 2.
[21] *Malbr. Manl.*, p. 336.
[22] *See* 'Pulicat' (*ante*) where 1612 is given as the date. Possibly the former date may be that of the settlement, the latter that of the fort.
[23] *Chingpt. Dt. Manl.*, p. 76; *Lists of Antiq.*, p. 173; Ref. Pls. xxxii, xxxiii, xxxiv, as to 'Castel Geldria.' In *Malbr. Manl.*, p. 336, 1610 is stated to be the date of settlement.
Mad. Manl. Admn., p. 139.
[25] *S. I. Palæ.*, p. 193.

In 1609 they concluded a formal treaty with the King of Kandy.

In 1611 the Spaniards drove the Dutch from Tidore and Banda.[26]

During the same year, the English Captain Hippon sailed up the east coast of India, and touched at several ports occupied by the Dutch, but found that trade with them was impossible. He arrived at Masulipatam and succeeded in founding an English factory there.[27] Their first efforts at trade were hindered by the native authorities, incited thereto by intrigues of the Dutch. In that year a ship, commanded by Hippon, who had with him as factor a Dutchman named Peter Williamson Floris, was despatched from Masulipatam by the Directors of the English East India Company to open trade along the east coast of India. They touched at Pulicat, but the Dutch effectually prevented any trade being conducted. In 1613 Floris returned to Masulipatam, and in July received some ambassadors from the King of Velur, who brought excuses for the offence given to the English at Paleakate (Pulicat) and made proposals for opening trade. "The Hollanders did all they could to obstruct these favours; but their influence was not great enough." In October news were received of the death of the king. "Great troubles were apprehended. The Hollanders were afraid of their castle newly built in Paleakate."[28]

In 1612 the Dutch were called in by the King of Kandy to assist him against the Portuguese, and in return they received the monopoly of the Ceylon cinnamon trade. They were to pay a yearly tribute to the king, but it is doubtful if it was ever rendered.

In the same year Timor was captured from the Portuguese.

In 1614 settlements were made at Masulipatam and in Siam. At the former place they took possession of the site and built a spacious fort as protection against encroachments by land and sea. They took every precaution to prevent the walls being undermined by inundation and paved the whole of the ditch. The quality of the work was of the best construction.[29]

In 1615 Sir Thomas Roe was sent by King James I. as the English ambassador to Jehangir's court, where he remained for about three years. Warning the English Company against the ruinous custom of maintaining unnecessary military forces, he wrote that "the Portugueses, notwithstanding their many rich residences, are beggared by keeping of soldiers, and yet their garrisons are but mean. They never made advantage of the Indies since they defended them. Observe this well. It has also been the error of the Dutch who seek plantations here by the sword. They turn a wonderful stock, they prole in all places, they possess some of the best, yet their dead pays consume all the gain."[30]

In 1617 they settled at Ahmadabad.[31]

In 1619, after a struggle with the English, they acquired the sovereignty of Java and built the city of Batavia, which subsequently became the chief seat of Government for their eastern possessions.

In this year a treaty was formed between England and Holland, whereby a 'Council of Defence' was constituted. It was composed of an equal number of members from the two companies. It was intended to settle any differences which might arise between them. But their rivalries were not to be so easily settled; they had before been all too frequent, and they continued unabated.[32]

---

[26] *Mad. Manl. Admn.*, pp. 2, 118.
[27] *Mad. Manl. Admn.*, p. 156.
[28] *God. Dt. Manl.*, p. 177.
[29] *Mad. Manl. Admn.*, pp. 2, 253.
[30] *Malbr. Manl.*, p. 340.
[31] *Malbr. Manl.*, p. 337.
[32] *Mad. Manl. Admn.*, pp. 2, 158.

In the same year a treaty was concluded between King James I. and the States-General, whereby the English Company were enabled to found a factory at Pulicat. It was erected in 1621–22 by the side of that of the Dutch, which had been built in 1609.

At this period was raised the largest joint-stock capital which had yet been collected in England. This increased the apprehensions of the Dutch, and matters grew worse, till they came to a climax at Amboyna in February 1623, when the English merchants were executed for an alleged conspiracy to seize the castle. By this act of annihilation they secured the complete monopoly of the spice trade.

In consequence of the oppression by the Dutch, it was found necessary to withdraw the English factory from Pulicat in 1622–23.[33]

At this period they were in the ascendant, and used their power to the detriment of the English. During 1620–22 they had temporary settlements in Persia and other places.[34]

In 1623 the privileges of the Dutch East India Company were renewed for a period of twenty-one years.[35]

In 1627 the trade in cloths from Masulipatam to the Eastern Archipelago was found so profitable, that the council at Batavia recommended that 300,000 rials in money should be sent to the town for carrying on the trade. These cloths were exchanged for gold, camphor and spices.

There was much rivalry and bad feeling between the Dutch and English factories at Masulipatam. In 1628 the latter were so harassed that they had temporarily to withdraw to Armegon. The factory was re-opened in 1632.[36]

In 1635 they took Formosa. In 1638 they united with the King of Kandy and made war on the Portuguese, with the intention of driving them from the Island of Ceylon. This result was attained at the end of the twenty years' war which ensued.[37]

In 1639 an attack was made on Goa.[38]

One of the oldest European acquisitions in the East is Malacca. It was taken by the Portuguese under Albuquerque in 1511. It remained in their possession till 1641, when, after being aided by the Achinese, the Dutch succeeded in taking it.

After this period, when the principal possessions in further India had been taken from the Portuguese, the Dutch directed their attention more particularly to India.

In 1643 the privileges of the Dutch East India Company were renewed by treaty for a further term of twenty-seven years.[39]

In 1647 the Dutch were trading at Sadras. It was famous for the muslins produced by its looms. The fort was built of brick and of some considerable strength.[40]

The first European account of the Brihaspati Cycle is the 'Open Deure' (1651) of Rogerius, Dutch Chaplain at Pulicat from 1631 to 1641.[41]

In 1652–53 ensued the naval war between England and Holland. On the arrival in Madras of news of the approaching war, representations were made that the extension of trade was impossible, unless Fort Saint George was strengthened. Instead of acceding to this, the Directors ordered the civil establishments to be reduced. In consequence of this, the inland wars, and the superior naval and military forces of the Dutch, the English settlements suffered and their trade declined.[42]

---

[33] *Chingpt. Dt. Manl.*, p. 142 ; M.J.L.S., 1879, p. 104 ; *Mad. Manl. Admn.* pp. 2, 156.
[34] *Malbr. Manl.*, p. 337. [35] *Mad. Manl. Admn.*, p. 159. [36] *Kist. Dt. Manl.*, pp. 89, 90, 99.
[37] *Mad. Manl. Admn.*, pp. 2, 118. [38] *Malbr. Manl.*, p. 337. [39] *Mad. Manl. Admn.*, pp. 31, 159.
[40] *Chingpt. Dt., Manl.*, p. 90 ; *Lists of Antiq.*, p. 189. [41] *S. I. Palæ.*, p. 73.
[42] *Mad. Manl. Admn.*, p. 162 ; *Malbr. Manl.*, p. 337.

In 1652 they built a factory at Palacole in the Gódávari district.[43]

In 1653 the Setupati of Ramnad rebelled and intrenched himself in the Island of Pamban. He was assisted by a number of Europeans who came in five vessels from Ceylon and Cochin. Their motive was said to be to gain a footing in the country.[44] They must have been either Portuguese or Dutch. They were most probably the latter, for, at that time, their activity was on the increase, and they were in search of new settlements. On the other side, the Portuguese power had declined, and they were unable to hold, and were rapidly losing even what settlements they then possessed. The remains of a fort of European construction still stand on the sea-shore at Pamban. It is known as the Dutch fort.

The war between the English and Dutch seriously impeded trade, and, at its termination, the claims of the former against the latter were submitted to arbitration. They included a sum for the heirs of the Englishmen massacred at Amboyna in 1623.

Colombo was taken from the Portuguese in 1655. From the time of their first appearance in Ceylon till the date when they expelled the Portuguese from the island three years later, the representatives of the two nations had been continually at war.[45]

In 1655 a settlement was made at Vingorla.[46]

In 1656 possession of Calicut was obtained from the Portuguese.[47]

In 1658 they expelled the Portuguese from their principal possessions in Ceylon and the Coromandel Coast. Jaffnapatam and Tuticorin were taken.[48]

In 1660 Negapatam was captured.[49] Negapatam became their chief settlement on the Coromandel Coast. To it were brought the commodities acquired by them in the course of their trade. These included iron, lead, copper, calico, linen, pepper and spices.[50]

After their settlement in Tuticorin, they acquired factories at Vambar, Vypar, Punnai Kayal, old Kayal, Manapar and Cape Comorin. They had also several stations in the interior, as Alwar-Tirunagari and Vadukankulam. The Portuguese had established Roman Catholic missions at Tinnevelly in 1532 and converted the Parávars. In 1542 the Missionary Xavier began his work. A Dutch Missionary named Baldaeus records, that in 1660, the Paravars then continued in the faith taught them by Xavier. Unlike the Portuguese, the Dutch claimed no authority over the Parava fishermen, but protected them against Hindu and Muhammadan oppression.[51]

The wars between the two powers had seriously impeded the efforts of the Catholic missionaries, and it was asserted that the Dutch persecuted the Catholics.[52]

It was also stated in Jesuit letters, that the Dutch in Tanjore, decoyed large numbers of Hindus from their homes, and sold them into slavery. But it is probable the statement is an exaggeration, and that they were only shipped as coolies.[53]

In 1661 Tangacheri was captured from the Portuguese. It had been held by the latter from 1519.[54]

The Dutch—who had been trying their fortunes at Surat—being dissatisfied with their prospects, and wishing for a place where they could pursue their vocation free from

---

[43] *Mad. Manl. Admn.*, p. 2.
[44] *Mdu. Cty.*, p. 129.
[45] *Tnvlly. Dt. Manl.*, pp. 45–47.
[46] *Malbr. Manl.*, p. 337.
[47] *Mad. Manl. Admn.* p. 2.
[48] *Mad. Manl. Admn.*, p. 2; *Tnvlly. Dt. Manl.*, pp. 45-47; *God. Dt. Manl.*, p. 196; *Lists of Antiq.*, p. 308.
[49] M.J.L.S. for 1879 and 1881, pp. 126 and 104–5; *Lists of Antiq.*, p. 281.
[50] *God. Dt. Manl.*, p. 196.
[51] *Tnvlly. Dt. Manl.*, pp. 45–47.
[52] *Mad. Manl. Admn.*, p. 626.
[53] *Mdu. Cty.*, p. 186.
[54] *Malbr. Manl.*, p. 338, and II, p. ccccxxii. *See* also M.J.L.S. for 1879, p. 127, where the dates are stated as 1555 to 1665.

competition with their successful English rivals, bethought themselves of searching for such a settlement. Cochin appeared to be such a place as they longed after, but it was held by the Portuguese. They, however, decided on expelling them, and an expedition was sent for the purpose under Van Goens. On the 12th March 1661, the Chief Minister to the Raja of Cochin entered into an agreement, to assist the Dutch commander in his attempt.

This agreement was ratified and dated on board the ship *De Muscaatboom*. On landing his forces, Van Goens fixed his head-quarters at the Bishop's house on the north of Cochin. He garrisoned the Roman Catholic church with eight hundred men, then embarked the remainder of his men and landed it on the south of the town. He seized a church in that quarter and made it his head-quarters. On the next day an unsuccessful attack was made on the fort. The siege was continued for some weeks; but, as the Raja of Purakkat was able to reinforce the garrison, the Dutch, for the time being, were forced to retreat. The Jews of the town, who had favoured the Dutch, were afterwards, on their departure, plundered by the Portuguese.[55]

In 1662 the Dutch took Cranganore, and returned to the attack of Cochin under Commander Hustart. The Portuguese made unsuccessful endeavours to prevent their landing from their ships. The head-quarters of the besiegers were fixed in the convent of St. John. In November, Van Goens joined them with a large reinforcement. In the month following, the Raja of Purakkat, who had previously succoured the Portuguese, arrived and placed supplies in the fort. The Dutch were thus compelled to bring up fresh troops. But the Portuguese still held out, and the Dutch, aided by the Raja of Cochin, kept up, by relays, for eight days and nights a continuous succession of assaults. The Portuguese were eventually wearied out, and their commander Pierre de Pon was obliged to surrender in the beginning of January 1663. Four hundred topasses, who had not been included in the terms of capitulation, and who, "knowing the cruel and licentious character of the Dutch soldiery in India," drew up at the gate out of which the defeated garrison were to pass, and stated they would massacre them all and fire the town if the same terms were not granted to them. Their demands were complied with; and some of them afterwards entered the Dutch service. The captors greatly improved the place and its trade; they erected quays, &c., and built many substantial houses in European style. They built another fort in place of that erected by the Portuguese. On taking possession, they found among the settlers, a small factory of the English East India Company, which had been settled there since 1634–35. The factors received immediate notice to leave, and they retired to Ponnáni. For many years, after they were thus unceremoniously removed, the English Company's servants had to rely for protection on the native chiefs in whose territories they settled. The Dutch also refused to allow the Carmelite missionaries and bishop to remain in the place, or exercise their ministry in Malabar. Afterwards, however, learning that they had nothing to dread from them, the prohibition was cancelled.[56] In 1664–65 the establishment of the English East India Company at Calicut was expelled by the Dutch.[57]

At this time, all the Portuguese possessions in Malabar fell to the Dutch.[58] In October 1664 the Company submitted to the States-General the following list of their settlements:—Amboyna; the Banda Islands; Pulo Roon; Ternate and other Moluccas;

---

[55] *Malbr. Manl.*, pp. 338–39.

[56] *Malbr. Manl.*, pp. 211, 338–40, and II, ccccxx. *Lists of Antiq.*, p. 254.

[57] M.J.L.S., 1879, p. 103; *Lists of Antiq.*, p. 246.

[58] *Mad. Manl. Admn.*, p. 2.

Macassar and Manado in Celebes; Timor; Bima on Sambawa; in Sumatra, Jambee, Palembang, and Indraghiri; Malacca; Tenasserim; Junk Ceylon; and factories in Tonquin, Arakan, Pegu, Ava and Sirian. On the Coromandel coast, at Pulicat, Tuticorin, Negapatam and Masulipatam. In Bengal, at Hoogly, Cossimbazaar, Dacca and Patna. A factory in Orissa. On the Malabar coast, at Cochin, Cranganore, Cannanore and Quilon. In Gujerat, at Surat and Ahmadabad. In Ceylon, at Colombo, Point de Galle, Negombo, Manaar and Jaffnapatam. In Persia and the Persian Gulf, Gambroon, Ispahan and Bassora. The Island of Mauritius. The Cape of Good Hope, Java, and some stations in Japan.[59]

In 1665 war broke out in Europe between England and Holland.[60]

In 1670 an alliance had been entered into between the English and French against the Dutch.[61]

The English East India Company re-established themselves at Calicut in 1668–69.[62]

In 1669 the Dutch drove the Portuguese out of St. Thomé.[63]

After the French had taken the Dutch settlement at Trincomalee Bay, and being thereafter in turn shortly expelled, they proceeded to St. Thomé, and in 1672 captured it from the Dutch.[64]

About 1670 Fernandez Navarette, a Dominican Friar, visited Masulipatam. He states that the English, Dutch, French and—some years before—the Danes had factories there. Some English and Dutch who had discharged themselves from their companies were settled there. He visited some of the English and Dutch, "because it was necessary," talked with them, and "found them very obliging in their words, and some no less in their actions."[65]

Philip Baldores, a Dutch Missionary from Ceylon, visited Masulipatam, and gives a description of its condition about 1672. "Masulipatam is a city seated near a large river, where the English and Dutch have their factories. It is very populous and the residence of a governor, who pays a certain yearly tribute to the King of Golconda, which he squeezes out of the inhabitants, specially the gentues, which are sorely oppressed by the Persians and Moors here, who farm all the weaving trade from the great persons; wherefore there is scarce any traficking here with profit unless you obtain a Patent from the king, which is not easy to be obtained, because the Governors (who pay 140,000 Pagodas of annual tribute to the king) constantly oppose it." This city is a place of great traffick, where most of our commodities, as also those transported hither from the Mologues, China, &c., are sold at a very good rate . . . . . . "Here is also a considerable traffick in Diamonds and Rubies."[66]

An interesting account of Dutch domestic life at this period in Masulipatam and the coast factories, is also given :—

"As the manner of Living of the vulgar sort among the Dutch in the East Indies is none of the best, so we will be satisfied with giving an account of those of the better sort. They commonly rise with the Sun—sleep after Sun-rising being accounted very unwholesome here in the morning. Some have a custom of washing their Heads, nay the whole Body, with cold Water, immediately after their coming out of bed; others do it with lukewarm Water three or four times a Week, the last of which I have found the best by Experience. Brandy or any other strong Liquors are not much used by the

[59] *Mad. Manl. Admn.*, p. 2. [60] *Malbr. Manl.* p. 342. [61] *Mad. Manl. Admn.*, pp. 164-5.
[62] M.J.L.S., 1879, p. 103; *Lists of Antiq.*, p. 246. [63] *Mad. Manl. Admn.*, p. 2. [64] *Mad. Manl. Admn.*, p. 173.
[65] *God. Dt. Manl.*, pp. 181–82; *Kist. Dt. Manl.*, pp. 90–91. [66] *Kist. Dt. Manl.*, p. 91.

wiser sort in the Morning, unless it be a spoonful just before Dinner, and a little at Night before they go to bed.

"The Tea (always used fasting by the Chineses) has got a mighty Ascendant over the Hollanders of late years. Its chief Virtues are to disperse the gross Vapours of the Head and Stomach, and consequently exhilarate our Spirits. The ordinary drink of the Hollanders is a mixture of water and sugar boiled together. Some fill certain Earthen Vessels overnight with Water, and add to it three or four Glasses of Spanish Wine, which, exposed together all night in the Dew turns white, and affords a pleasant Liquor, but is a little too cool, for which reason some put a certain quantity of Mum in the Vessel. The Brunswick Mum is both more pleasant and wholesome here than in Europe. Among the wines those of Spain are most in request. It's true they sometimes inflame the Gall, but against that they make use of Rhubarb and Cremor of Tartar. The French and Rhenish Wines are not strong enough in these hot Countries, where the stomach requires more lively cordials, as a little Brandy, or a moderate share of Canary. Their ordinary Food is Goats, Sheep, Fowl, Hares, Peacocks and such like.

"The Hollanders most generally take their Afternoon's sleep here, as the Italians and some other Europeans do in hot countries, a thing sufficiently commendable in the Indies, where the heat of the Sun Beams invites the inhabitants to pass away the middle of the Day (when they are unfit for Business) at their ease. They have also a constant custom of washing their mouths after Dinner. About 3 or 4 a clock in the Afternoon, they take their Tea, and after that a Walk; the Evenings and Nights being pretty cool and very pleasant here, especially when the Moon shines. They sup commonly about 7 or 8 a clock, but very moderately, and go to sleep about 10 or 11 upon Quilts, Feather-beds being not used in the Indies." [67]

Fifty years later, or about 1723, Canter Visscher says that "for strong drink in general the Portuguese have no taste; the Dutch, on the contrary, drink to such an extent as to expose themselves to the reproaches of the Portuguese and the natives; the English are liable to the same imputation." [68]

The Dutch settlements on the Malabar Coast in 1673 were Cochin, Cannanore, Cranganore, Quilon and Calli Quilon, with the Governor's seat at the former.[69]

During the war between the English and Dutch, a fleet of the latter, carrying 6,000 men under Commander Van Goens, threatened the settlements of the former at Bombay, but so efficient a defence was offered, that the attack was abandoned. Later, two English ships were captured by them off Masulipatam.[70]

On the English deciding to try and get a settlement in the Gingee country, it was stated in favour of the proposal that "one of the main reasons why the Dutch keep so many factories upon this coast, which being divided into several governments, if they be obstructed in their business by one Governor, they have another place to find." [71]

In the Minutes of Consultation of the Madras agency in 1673–4 are recorded the particulars of the first English settlement in the Gingee country. Muhammad Khan, the Governor of Gingee, requested that an Englishman or two, and a half score of peons might be sent to take possession of the places selected, "to set up the English flag and hold it, freeing him from the importunities of the French and Dutch." [72]

In 1674 the country was rented out to the Naiks. Those of Pallavaram and Chingleput—who are described as friends of the English—were proceeding to a marriage at Golconda, and it was considered advisable to make them suitable presents. The Poonamalee renter about this time was one not easily satisfied, and the English refusing to comply with one of his demands, he—during his visit to Golconda—brought

[67] *God. Dt. Manl.*, p. 198.
[68] *Mad. Manl. Admn.*, p. 445.
[69] *Malbr. Manl.*, p. 342.
[70] *Ibid.*
[71] *S. Arcot. Dt. Manl.*, p. 18.
[72] *S. Arcot. Dt. Manl.*, p. 15.

to the notice of the court the growing importance of the English and their insolent independence.

He contrasted their conduct with the servility of the French and the Dutch at Pulicat and Sadras.[73]

After the French and English had entered into an alliance, the Dutch in 1674 came to recover St. Thomé from the French. They picked a quarrel with Fort Saint George for sheltering some Frenchmen from Java and "Monsieur Peter Deltor, second for affairs of the Royal Company of France at Metchlipatam." The Dutch and Muhammadans, who were threatening the Fort, demanded that they be removed. The Governor hesitated to comply, and the Frenchmen wished to be permitted to go to St. Thomé, but the Dutch and Muhammadans refused. It was anticipated that the Dutch fleet would attack Fort Saint George, whose defences were weak and undermanned. The Frenchmen were ultimately escorted to Bijapur. In August of that year, the French surrendered St. Thomé to the Dutch under Van Goens. Siege would thereafter have doubtless been laid to Fort Saint George, but for the arrival of the news of peace between England and Holland the preceding January.[74]

Most of the surviving French proceeded to Surat, but about sixty of them, headed by François Martin, went to Pondicherry, where they obtained a small piece of land, and were permitted to erect a fort.[75]

Negapatam was formally conveyed to the Dutch by Vijaya Raghava, the last of the Telugu Nayak Princes of Tanjore. The extinction of this dynasty has been placed at 1674–5. The Mahratta Prince Ekoji, in 1676, confirmed the grant made by his predecessor. Both deeds are executed on silver plates now preserved in the Museum at Batavia.[76]

In a memorandum dated 1676 for the personal conduct of the young men of the English factory at Masulipatam, the following interesting items are found among the rules to be observed :—

"III. For learning the Portugull languages : That the Company pay a Tutor six months : the Tutor to read to them one hower every day of the weeke ; the time to be after dinner, whilst they are all together ; if any absent or neglect to forfeit : that account be kept of the forfeitures ; that if they be not at six months end perfect, then three months more to be allowed ; wherein he that speakes not the language shall forfeit for every time that he speakes English : the forfeitures to goe towards payment of the Tutor and what they fall short to make up among themselves. The like for learning the Mores languages. The account of forfeitures to be sent to the Company which will more affect than the loss of the money.

"IV. In case they will not be conformed to rules, that they may be sent to the Fort and kept there. The Dutch send all such young men as will not be regulated to Batavia, and make them serve for soldiers till their time expire."[77]

In 1677 the Dutch instigated the Javanese to attack the English factory at Bantam, and the agent of the latter was killed.[78]

Sivaji, the Mahratta chief, on his invasion of the Coromandel coast, passed by Madras, and there were constant rumours that he was about to attack the English and Dutch settlements. He, however, retired after taking the fortress of Gingee in 1677.[79]

---

[73] *Chingpt. Dt. Manl.*, p. 144.
[74] *Kist. Dt. Manl.*, p. 99 ; *Mad. Manl. Admn.*, pp. 3, 157, 164-5.
[75] *S. Arcot Dt. Manl.*, p. 16 ; *Malbr. Manl.*, p. 342.
[76] *S.I. Palæ.*, pp. 56, 93.
[77] *Kist. Dt. Manl.*, p. 93.
[78] *Mad. Manl. Admn.*, p. 157.
[79] *Mad. Manl. Admn.*, p. 166.

The Dutch and French had been competing for settlements in the Gingee country; and the former had built factories at Porto Novo and Devanapatam near Cuddalore. When they first settled at Devanapatam, there existed a small fort, which had been taken possession of by the Mahrattas when they captured Gingee. The French endeavoured to outbid them, and prevented their securing it. The incident is described in the following extract from the Madras Government records:—

"Difference between Sevajce people and the Dutch.

"27. Some of Sevajees people being sent to the Govern^{r} of Pollicat to treat about Passes for ships goeing from Porto Novo: which the Dutch have refused to give and therefore are upon withdrawing their Factory at Tefnapatam in that part of Sevajees new conquests, which he has given to his Brother Santogee, the said persons passed by here in their returne and delivered a letter from Sevagees Chief Minister a Bramah to Verona wherein he intreated him to interpose and use his interest for a good accomodation betweene the Dutch and them, which was seconded by the Messengers who informed Verona that the Govern^{r} of Pollicatt had given them a flatt denyall, saying that such were the orders from Battavia from which he durst not vary, and Verona told them he could not concerne himselfe at all therein with which ansswear they departed. The new Generall and Councell at Battavia have made very great alterations amongst the Dutch upon the Coast this yeare, in changeing their Imployements and abateing and cutting off of their Qualletys, sallorys and allowances, whereupon many of them, and those of the ablest men amongst them are so discontented that they have left their present imployments and taken their passage to Battavia. In the beginning of this month there arrived 6: or 8: great ships said to be men of warr upon the Coast about Toffnapatam, Porto Novo and Pullichere and the Dutch at their ffactory at Toffnapatam did then imediately imbarque all their goods, lumber and weomen and sent them away to Pollicat, the Chief and two or three men only staying in the ffactory, and the Govern^{r} at Pollicatt gave notice to all their merchants the Natives that if they had any goods or moneys and their familys in that part of Sevagees Country they should draw all out from thence as fast as they could and thereupon they did gett all their familys away and their estates as well as they could, it was then reported that the Dutch had a design to take off the Ffrench at Pullichere and to take the Castle at Teffnapatam (wch they were upon buying of Sevagee the last yeare but the French outbid them for it) and tis said they had put their men into Boates to land them at Pullicheree, but finding the French provided to receive them they returned aboard again without doeing anything and at Teffnapatam Sevagees people having noticed of the designe, had put more men into the Castle and provided for their defence, for this Expedition there were severall Boates, mussoolads, men and abundance of Amunition and provisions sent off from Pollicatt with all secrecy and hast, but tis now said all is come to nothing and that those men of Warr are gone to Taffnapatam.

Of the Dutch affairs.

Their attempt upon Pullichere and Teffnapatam.

"28. About ten dayes since came hither Capt. Wilkins Wigbert in the Danes service, having been Resident for that Company at Metchlep^{a} about a yeare, was now returning to Trincumbar, for whose accomodation the Govern^{r} of that place had sent a sloope upon w^{h} Capt. Wigbert had laden all his goods and necessarys and was at Pollicat with said sloope intending himselfe there to imbarque upon her, and having dispatched all things in order to his goeing aboard, went into a boat of a Dutch ship there about 8: a clock at night to goe aboard ye sloope, but the Boat rowed up and downe all the road over and could not find the sloope, the next morning allsoo she was not to be soone, whereupon Capt. Wigbert came away hither supposing the sloope might be come to this place, but here was noe Acco^{tt} to be learnt of her, and now he hath advice from Pollicat that there was a sloope put in at Careda and a white man came ashoare for water and she was put to sea againe, and that there was the Corps of a Black supposed to be one of Capt. Wigberts servants that was in the sloope cast upon ye shoare at Pollicat with his hands and leggs bound with a Caire Rope, whereupon tis much to be feared that the men of the sloope being 8 Danes a Boy and a Dutch Pilot (that went on board her out of a Dutch ship in Pollicatt Road and a fellow that has formerly been guilty of great villanys) have run away with the sloope, there

Of a Danes Sloope run away with by the men.

being a considerable value of goods and monys aboard her, this Captaine Wigbert acknowledges to have of his own there to the vallue of 9,000 pag^{os} and all his apparell, &c., soo that he had not left him any thing but what was upon his body."[80]

In 1679, on account of some dissensions among the English Company's servants in their northern Factories, the Agent of Fort Saint George proceeded on an official tour of inspection of the settlements. The chief point of his visit seems to have been Masulipatam, where he came in contact with, and gives some particulars of the Dutch officials and their settlements—

"26th March. The Chief of the Dutch, Signor Outhorne, sent to excuse his not visiting the Agent to-day by reason of business in dispatching a ship for Battavia, and desired to make his visit to-morrow,

"27th. In the afternoon, the Chief of the Dutch with his second and five more came to visit the Agent, &c., who were entertained at a Banquett and went home againe about 8 at night. Signor Outhorne discoursing with the Agent amongs other Bravadoos delivered this as remarkable, that their Company had soe many Island and Castles in the South Seas, many of which he named, that they were as Emperors, they had heretofore made kings, as a king of Ternot and a king of Cochin, and now lately they had made an Emperor, viz., the Mataran, who had severall kings under him, and he had given their Company all the sea-ports upon the coast of Java, when they wanted men, upon their call, the kings brought their armies to fight for them, as a great Prince of Macape, whom he named had brought a great army to Battavia to fight the king of Bantam by land, and they intended to block it up by sea, and when 'twas objected that it may be their company at home would not approve of a warr with Bantam, he replied he knew better for he came from Battavia this yeare about January last."

This boastful language was in keeping with the ostentatious assumption of superiority the Dutch officials assumed. They had as yet a firmer hold of the country than their competitors the English. The remarks foreshadowed the attack on Bantam some years later.

"METCHLEPATAM,
"*April 5th, 1679.*

"The Gazettes which came to our hands we alsoe send you herewith, by which you will be advised that the peace was signed between France and the Dutch upon the 31st July but the later advices say that those affairs are uncertain by reason of a fierce battle fought between the French and the Prince of Orange in which about 12,000 men were slaine after the Peace was signed.

"In the evening we went and supd at the Dutch garden which is about halfe a mile distance from the English garden, where the Dutch have two houses to which they often retire out of Towne for better aire which is alsoe much wanting in the English garden.

"9th. In the evening the Agent tooke a view of the house, warehouses, outhouses, garden and yards which are all well scituated upon the side of the great River that goes into the sea about five miles from the Factory, the townes of Madapollam and Narsapore joyne together, the Dutch house for their Iron worke in Narsapore being a little above muskett shott from the English Factory in Madapollam, Narsapore lyes below Madapollam downe the River, and that place is under the Governour of Metchlepatam and has the command of all the River for the customes as far as Corango, but Madapollam, Mellick, Mahmudpet and Naurasporam, tho they all joyne together to Narsapore, yet they have every one distinct Havaldars for the gathering the ground rent independent from Narsapore or Metchlepatam at present.

"10th. The Agent visited Narsapore. At our returne home from Naurasporam about noone your Dutch Chief of Pollicull being this morning come thence to their house at Narsapore where their Flagg was hoisted up, sent to desire to give the Agent a visit this evening which was admitted, they came about 4 a clock were treated at a collation and went away about 8 at night to Pollicull very much importuning the Agent to give them a visitt at Pollicull—they told us that one who aforetime was King of Orixa was risen with a great army of 35,000 Horse upon your coast and country of Gingerlee, who

[80] *Pub. Consultations*, Vol. II, for the year 1678—1679. General No. 2, 154, Fort St. George, September 1678.

had besieged the Seer Lascar or Gratt of the king of Gulcondah in a Castle and had taken away 500 laest of Pady of the Dutch Companys."

The information evidently referred to the attack and capture by the Mahrattas of the fortress of Gingee—

"Pollicull ye Agent &ca., went to visit the Dutch at Pollicull.

"14th. The Agent, &ca., went to visit the Dutch at Pollicull this evening wch is about 7 miles inland from Madapollam, there the Dutch have a ffactory of a large compound where they Dye much Blew Cloth, having above 300 : Jars set in the ground for that worke, alsoe they make many their best paintings there, the Towne being first rented by them at 2,000 : old pagos ℘. Ann : is now given them free by the King and they say they make 4,000 : pagos ℘ Ann1 of it and sometimes more, at Pollicullis a great Pagoda where great numbers of People come to worship once a yeare, and performe their vowes of being hung up by the skin of the back with Iron Hookes at the end of a long Pole turned round upon a post of about 10 : or 12 : feet high before the pagodae. This feast hapened this yeare the day after we were at Pollicull, and some of our people went to it, and saw near 20 : people soo hung up by the back before the pago at the top of the high pole." [81]

"16th. We went to view the Dutch house and compound at Narsapore which is a very large piece of ground divided into two large inclosed quadrangles, in one of which is as many forges as 300 smiths may worke in them, the compound reaches downe to the River side upon the sandy banke of which lyes many vessells which are imployed in that great Rice trade of Gingerlee." [82]

In August of the same year, the agent made a second visit to Masulipatam. "They arrived in the Masulipatam roads on the forenoon of August 4th, finding there a great Dutch fly-boat which saluted them, a small ship of a Dutch freeman of Ceylon" and some junks.

On the 6th of the month, the agent warned the Factories to be frugal in their expenses, "the Dutch having last yeare put away their Drums, Pipes, &c., and many Peons."

Regarding the Dutch, he wrote— "at Metchlepatam the Dutch have landed this yeare a very large stock of silver, copper and spices, wherewith it is reported they intend to carry out vast investments to the prejudice of the English business, having advanced 10 per cent. of the usuall prices of all sorts of calicoes and with the gold coined some months past at Pullicatt paid off all their debts on the coast, and do now in all their Factories make their investments with ready money advances, which they never did heretofore."

The ship conveying the agent again anchored at Masulipatam on the 13th January 1680, and in the afternoon the agent went ashore. "The Dutch chief stood upon the Terras of their house when we passed by, but came not downe to meet us in the street. He sent next day to say that he would visit the agent who asked to be excused on account of press of business." [83]

The following extract from the Madras Government records, makes a quaint reference to contemporary events, which would in these later times find a fitting place in the public press :—

"Munday the 27 Mr. John Bridger not comming to Towne, it being very foule weather, and Mr. Timothy Wilkes being sick, the Councell mett not.

"30. This day came newse of the death of Jaques Caulier, Director for the Netherlands East India

The death of Jaques Caulier Governour of the Castle Geldria at Paliacat.

Compa on the Coast of Choromandell and Governour of their Castle Geldria at Paliacat, he departed this life the 25th Detto :, and was buryed ye extday, the Extraordinary great Raines wch hath fallen, hath so swallen the Rivers that before this day, no one man could come from Paliacatt hither." [84]

---

[81] *Pub. Records* April, 1679, p. 169.

[82] *Kist. Dt. Manl.*, pp. 130—150 ; *God. Dt. Manl.*, pp. 185-86.

[83] *Kist. Dt. Manl.*, p. 97 ; *God. Dt. Manl.*, p. 190.

[84] *Pub. Records*, Oct. 1679, p. 181; *See* also plate xxvii and page 59, where the date differs. The time mentioned in the records, must have been founded on a rumour, prior to the actual event.

The Dutch Factory at Masulipatam was probably chiefly engaged in manufacturing into chintzes, and exporting the cloth woven at Palkole. Their exports from the east coast were stated to amount to £43,750, but the profits were lost in the expenses of their garrisons. [85] They latterly began to realize this, and in various ways tried to reduce unproductive expenditure. Their efforts in this direction at Masulipatam have before been noted. On the west coast, they gravely considered the propriety of destroying, or reselling to the Portuguese, the forts of Cannanore, Cranganore, and Quilon; the negotiations did not succeed, and the resolution was never carried out. The Dutch—as has before been remarked, in their connection with the east coast,—were intolerant of those professing Roman Catholicism, and one of their reasons alleged for wishing to rid themselves of these places, was, that this faith had obtained a firm hold on the people. [86]

In 1680 the Dutch appear to have returned to Porto Novo, whence they had departed two years previously, and to have got a grant of land from the Maharattas, with permission to build a factory. [87]

In 1682 the Dutch took Bantam, and drove out the English. [88] That this event had been long in contemplation, was shown by others which happened previously, and by the remarks of the Dutch Chief at Masulipatam in 1679, when visiting the English agent there.

After the failure of negotiations with the Portuguese in regard to the disposal of certain of the Dutch possessions on the west coast, the Roman Catholic priests who had been banished therefrom, were in 1684, allowed to return to their flocks. [89]

In 1686, the Dutch in Masulipatam considered they had been insulted by the King of Golconda, and took forcible possession of the town. They, thereon put restrictions on the English trade "on purpose to lay the English low in the Eyes of the Natives, according to their usual treatment." The Dutch Governor at Pulicat announced the capture, to the English Government at Fort Saint George, in a document signed by John Pitts, Johannes Huysman and Rehneir Jacobson. "It cannot be unknown to your Honours, how our Honourable Netherlands East India Company, for some years on this coast of Choromandel . . . . . are abused and affronted in many unspeakable manners . . . . . whereupon the Right Honourable Council of India cannot swallow such innumerable overgrown injuries and have been forced to resolve the better to come by our right . . . . . to take in possession (by the forces now sent us) the city of Metchlepatam . . . . and by God's blessing and the Companie's Arms, so effected that we now for our Company this 26th of July are masters of the aforesaid city of Metchlepatam; wherein, according to our Orders and to the maintaining our Friendships, we shall not incommode or hinder Your Honours to imbarque in your ships . . . . what goods you have ready by you as you have occasion, and to disimbarque all your Provisions and Merchandize which are brought by your ships to Metchlepatam, and lay them up in your Factory; but not to carry them without the city to dispose of them to Merchants or Subjects of the King of Gulcondah, so long as our Company hath not satisfaction from the king and keep possession of the Towne."

The Council of Fort Saint George replied that they had received "a large Declaration from Your Honours of the State," and because they were ignorant of the causes of the war, they could say nothing to it, "but we are not ignorant of your farther design therein, and we wish it may not be your design to overthrow the Right Honourable

---

[85] *God. Dt. Manl.*, pp. 196, 198. [86] *Malbr. Manl.*, pp. 342–43. [87] *S. Arcot. Dt. Manl.*, p. 17.
[88] *Mad. Manl. Admn.*, p. 157. [89] *Malbr., Manl.*, p. 343.

Company's Trade there, which has been practised already too much, particularly at Bantam, for we have observed that, in all your contracts with the Kings and Princes of these countries you endeavour to exclude our Trade in their Ports." But they must tell the Dutch that they knew of no obligation to receive or observe such directions, and as the Factory was their own property, they would follow their trade as hitherto, "and we shall not want them that are appointed to give us an account of the least obstruction thereto, which we advise you not to do, because of the ill-consequences that may be to your own interests."

The Dutch tried to justify their action, and stated that the English merchants had of their own accord retired from the town for fear of their property being burnt. The English had also "divers other Lodges more, by or not far from Metchlepatam, where they could, without any molestation, drive their Trade." [90]

In 1687 the English and the Emperor Aurangzib were at war in Bengal, and, in July of that year, the troops of the latter advanced as far south as the Kondapalle fort, when the Dutch, French and English temporarily deserted Masulipatam.[91]

In 1689 war broke out between France and Holland. After the revolution of 1688, which placed William of Orange on the English throne, English and Dutch interests in India became parallel; and in 1690 the combined fleets of the two nations fought an indecisive battle with that of the French off Madras.[92]

In 1690 the Madras agency was treating for the purchase of the Fort of Devanapatam. The price at first demanded was high; and it was decided to try and get it lowered for the English, or raised to the Dutch and the French, who were also offering for it. An agreement was come to for its purchase by the English, with all the land within gun-shot distance. The only exception was the Dutch factory and town, and town of Cuddalore. The fort was afterwards known as Fort Saint David. At the time of its purchase, the Dutch had a factory and some buildings at Devanapatam. They assisted at the transfer and demarcation of the fort and land; and at the time made no claim to ownership of any part of it.

In 1691 they began to assert a right to Manjakupam; they threatened to convert their factory into a fort, and bring forces from their other factories and mass them there. They secured the co-operation of the Subedar, who wrote to Madras, that Devanapatam and Manjakupam were outside the limits of the English fort, and the Dutch were not to be molested.

On this, the Madras Agency took an affidavit from the two officers who had conducted the purchase, and sent a copy of it, accompanied by a letter of instructions, to the Deputy Governor of the fort. They gave orders to seize Manjakupam by force, if necessary, should the Dutch still refuse to rent it from him on the same terms as they had hitherto done from the Diwan. The following is the letter referred to :—

(Dated 21st July 1691 from the Council, to the Deputy Governor of Fort Saint David.)

"As to your disputes with your unreasonable neighbours the Dutch, we have endeavoured all fair ways to gain them satisfaction therein.

"but by their insinuations and bribes they take the advantage of a variable necessitous Prince to dishonour his words and deeds, to deprive the Right Honourable Company and nation of their just

---

[90] *God. Dt. Manl.*, p. 201; *Kist. Dt. Manl.*, pp. 104–5. [91] *Kist. Dt. Manl.*, p. 105.
[92] *Mad. Manl. Admn.*, p. 170; *Ch. Dt. Manl.*, p. 148.

purchast rights, tho' as the Dutch argue for themselves, that Rama Raja had no power to sell their factory . . . . had the Dutch the least pretence to such a right they would have declared it at its being delivered into our possession,

". . . . they acknowledge they duly paid two and a half per cent. custom at the time of our purchase and possession and that they were only renters of Mangee Copang,

". . . . . the mercenary Morattaes who no doubt may be tamper'd and induc'd by bribes to resell the fort too ten times over to the same or severall persons,

". . . . . that notwithstanding their underhand dealings and many bribes received from the Dutch in this business the king by them now offers . . . . . to resell to us Mangee Copang and Tegnapatam exclusive of all Dutch pretences and company too,

". . . . . Mangee Copang is the Right Honourable Company's just purchase, therefore take possession of it, except the Dutch will agree to pay to you the same rent they paid the Duan,

". . . . . then for the Dutch customes let it be the same they usually paid the Duan, which if they refuse then deny them the boat and people, to serve them, giving them notice that what goods are or shall be landed within your precincts without your license are seizable and shall be confiscated to the Right Honourable Company as Lords Proprietors of the place.

". . . . . We doubt the Dutch will make a clamour at your coyning their pagodas and decry them all they can, however, make the experiment, but be sure to equall them in all respects both in fineness and weight and stamp, and we shall give them all the reputation we can here and to the southward. . . . ."

Towards the end of August 1691 Manjakupam was seized; and the Dutch chief at Devanapatam boasted that, as soon as some expected soldiers arrived, he would recover it, float the Dutch flag and defend it. Thereafter a Union Jack was sent to the English Deputy Governor, with orders to pitch it at Manjakupam, mount a guard over it, and defend it by force if necessary; but the matter ended here.[93]

In September 1691 the Dutch handed over Chetwai to the Zamorin.[94]

During the course of the war between Holland and France, the former sent a fleet of nineteen vessels against Pondicherry in 1693. After a siege of twelve days Martin the Governor was obliged to surrender on the 5th September. The captors improved the fort and made it one of the strongest in India.[95]

In 1695 the notorious Captain Kydd captured a small Dutch bark, and carried it off to Madagascar.[96]

By the treaty of Ryswick in 1697, peace was proclaimed between Holland and France; and two years later, Pondicherry was handed back to the latter power. The French Chief François Martin, who had founded, and been obliged to surrender it, again took possession. The Dutch demanded 16,000 pagodas for improvements to the fortifications effected during the term of their occupancy.[97]

In 1697 owing to the penurious policy entered on, the walls of the Cochin fort had fallen into a state of dilapidation. In accordance with the declaration of 1680, for curtailing their military expenditure, the forts at Cochin, Cannanore and Quilon were reduced in size, and the troops at Paponetty, Purakkat and Calli-Quilon withdrawn. The marine establishment was reduced to a small yacht, two sloops and three rowing boats. These reductions resulted in lowering Dutch prestige in the eyes of the native powers.[98]

The various companies were not only jealous of each other, but more so of any one—even though their countryman, but not of their company—who attempted to gain a footing

---

93 *S. Arcot Dt. Manl.*, pp. 22, 28, 30–33.

94 *Malbr. Manl.*, pp. 343–4.

95 *Mad. Manl. Admn.*, pp. 3, 170, 173.

96 *Malbr. Manl.*, p. 74.

97 *S. Arcot Dt. Manl.*, p 36; *Mad. Manl. Admn.*, p. 3.

98 *Malbr. Manl.*, pp. 343–4.

in or open trade with the country. Non-official Europeans could only move about with a permit, and every obstacle was placed in the way of outside vessels touching at their ports.

Abstract.

" To

the Worp: [a] Peter Van Singelans Chief for affairs of the Rt. Hon: Netherlands East India Comp: [a] en Pollicatt &c.—Councille.

That it is true that 3 Europeans were permitted to go to Pollicatt. That a certain Chetty will be sent to Pollicatt to give evidence in a certain case as soon as he returns from Sadrappatam.

Yr very affect' friends,
NATH: HIGGINSON.
JOHN STYLEMAN.
FRANCIS ELLIS.
THOMAS WRIGHT
MATT: EIMPSON.
EDWD: TREDCROFT." [99]

" To

The Worsp[ll] Peter Van Singelans Chief for affaires of the Rt: Honb[le] Netherlands East India Company &c., Councill in Pollicatt.

No. 94.

We are this day informed that yesterday a ship with English Colours, Anchored in Pollicatt road and that two persons belonging to this said ship came ashore to your Factory. The same ship did on the 11th Instant in like manner anchor in St. Thoma Road; from whence we have been informed by some, that she was suspected to be a Pirate, and by others that she was an Interloper passing under the name of the Resolution Captain Ethrington Commander. Wee know not whether said ship bee a Pirate or Interloper. But we know that she doth not belong to the Rt: Hon: English East India Company, and therefore their coming into India is highly prejudiciall to the Trade of both Companys in India. For prevention whereof our Honble: Masters do inform us, they have made an Agreement with the Rt: Honble: Netherlands East India Company that their servants shall not trade wth any pretended English ships that shall come to any of their Ports or Factoryes in India without a certificate the form whereof for your more certain information comes inclosed.—

In consideration whereof and of the strict alliance betwixt our nations, and the good understanding that hath been for so long maintained between our Companys, wee doubt not but Your Worship &c. will readily comply with the purport of the forementioned Agreement, and you will receive orders from the Honble: Governour and Councill of Negapatam unto whom wee now write—

Wee
Remain.
Your very affect: friends.
NATH: HIGGINSON.
JOHN STYLEMAN.
FRANCIS ELLIS.
THOMAS WRIGHT.
MATT: EIMPSON.
EDWD: TREDCROFT." [100]

FORT ST. GEORGE,
18th June 1698.

" To

The Honble: Lawrence Pitt Councill Extraordinary of India and Gover[nr] of Negapatam &c., Coast Choromandell for Affaires of the Rt: Honble: Netherlands East India Company and Councill.

No. 97.

---

[99] *Letters from Fort St. George*, Vol. VIII, p. 137, No. 81, 1698.

[100] *Letters from Fort St. George*, 1698, Vol. VIII, p. 156.

We are this day informed that a ship with English Colours did Anchor yesterday in Pollicatt Road, concerning which we have wrote to Letter to the Worp[l]: Chiefe and Councill, whereunto wee may your Hon[r] &c. to bee referred, and give such orders as you shall think necessary for the prevention of that mischief which hath arisen to the Trade of both Companys by such Piraticall or Interloping ships frequenting India.

Wee have reason to suspect the said will proceed further northward, we therefore pray your Hon[r] &c. that you will please to give your Orders, allso to your other Factories in these parts so Commending Your Honour &c., to Gods protection.

Wee Remain.
Your Hon[rs] &c. affection[t]
Friends and humble servants.

FORT ST. GEORGE,
18th June 1698.

NATH: HIGGINSON.
JOHN STYLEMAN.
FRANCIS ELLIS.
THOMAS WRIGHT.
MATT: EIMPSON.
EDWD: TREDCROFT."[101]

CHAPTER III.

EIGHTEENTH CENTURY, TO WITHDRAWAL OF OPERATIONS IN INDIA.

FROM an early period of their settlement on the south-east coast of India, the Dutch had obtained from the king of Madura the monopoly of the pearl fishery off the Tinnevelly coast. They drew a considerable revenue in licenses. These were granted at the rate of 60 ecus per vessel. A considerable profit was also derived from the conch fishery. The manner in which they conducted the pearl fishery in 1700, is described in the letters of a Jesuit missionary of that date. It is practically the method followed at the present day.

About this time they sent an embassy to the Setupathi of Ramnad, with valuable presents to induce him to secure to them his right to the pearl fishery on his coasts; but they gained nothing thereby.

Their ordinary trade in this quarter was in cloths from Madura, for which Japan leather and Malacca spices were exchanged.

Tuticorin was the only harbour on that part of the coast, where a European vessel could weather the stormy season. It is described as a flourishing town of over fifty-thousand inhabitants. The Dutch had built a small fort for the protection of their trade, and several commodious and handsome store-houses. The town looked well from the sea, but on closer inspection it was found to consist almost entirely of mud huts.

A letter of Father Martin in 1700 states, that the Parava Christians were much persecuted by the Dutch, who had also expelled the Goanese priests from Tuticorin and Negapatam.[102]

In 1701 the Dutch proposed to take possession of an old English factory at Conimere, which, along with that at Cuddalore, had been withdrawn in 1691; but the English objected, and the design was abandoned.[103]

The withdrawal of the Dutch from Chetwai in 1691, gave the Zamorin the desired opportunity of being placed in a position to annoy the Cochin Raja; and, in consequence,

---

[101] *Letters from Fort St. George*, 1698, Vol. VIII, p. 159. [102] *Tiny. Dt. Manl.*, pp. 45, 60–61; *Madura Country*, p. 227.
[103] *S. Arcot Dt. Manl.*, p. 37; *Mad. Manl. Admn.*, p. 170.

the Dutch were, from 1701 to 1710, caused much profitless expenditure through the desultory warfare they were drawn into in defence of the interests of the latter. Through the continuance of these hostile attacks, the Raja of Cochin made over to the Dutch such claims as he had on the island; and they, in 1714, proceeded to erect a fort on the north of it. The Zamorin, on the advice of the chief of the English factory, decided to circumvent them. Some soldiers were sent, disguised as coolies, who secured employment as workmen on the erection of the fort. One evening they overpowered the sentinels, and took possession of the partly erected fort. The Dutch withdrew their men and sailed for Cochin. While engaged in doing so, the English colours were hoisted on the spot, through the English factor having obtained permission from the Zamorin to erect a warehouse on Chetwai. The Zamorin then demolished the works. The Dutch were incensed at the insult, and sent a force which recovered Chetwai and Paponetty. The Zamorin was forced to re-build the fort and to pay other large sums in compensation. The Dutch formally resumed possession in April 1717. It was named Fort William, and Heer Wilhelm Blasser was appointed commandant.[104]

A Protestant mission school was founded by Ziegenbalg at Cuddalore in 1717.[105]

As a consequence of the expensive wars into which the Dutch had been drawn in their support of the Raja of Cochin against the Zamorin, the Supreme Council in Batavia in 1721, decided that the former was no longer to receive their support. In informing him of the fact, he was solemnly cautioned to live peaceably with all men.[106]

In 1724 the town, fort, and dependencies of Malacca, Singapore, which had already been occupied for some years, and the Dutch settlements in India which had been ceded by treaty to England by the Netherlands King in exchange for Bencoolen and Sumatra, were transferred to the English East India Company.[107]

The jealousy among the various European Companies, and their striving after aggrandizement, led to the strained relations so continuously displayed in their mutual dealings. At other times, nominally at peace with each other, and abstaining from the open hostility of war, they nevertheless attempted to gain their ends by inciting the native powers to revolt, and assisted them with the means to carry it out. Even in cases where they may not have been the inciting cause, they seized the opportunity of a revolt, to gain by bonds for sums advanced, a hold over part of the territory of some necessitous prince. The English themselves, though having reason to resent such tactics, were not averse, or were perchance forced by circumstances to adopt similar means. In some of their disputes in Malabar in 1726, they resolved to assist the native powers with money "as being cheaper than war."[108]

In 1727 the Dutch still retained possession of Fort Angelo at Cannanore. The town is described as a large one, built at the foot of the bay. It was then independent of them, and under the Mappila Raja Ali who lived under the protection of their fort.

The chief aim of the Portuguese—who were ousted by the Dutch—had been the destruction of the Moorish commerce. In their efforts in this direction, they succeeded in permanently injuring the town of Calicut as a seaport, and diverting its trade to other ports. The Dutch adopted other methods, took the Moors under their protection, and used them for the furtherance of their own trade. They set up the Mappila chief to seize Codally, in order that they might secure the pepper trade of the country. They

---

104 *Malbr. Manl.*, pp. 350, 496, 666; M.J.L.S., 1879, p. 116.
105 *Mad. Manl. Admn.*, p. 624.
106 *Malbr. Manl.*, p. 351.
107 M.J.L.S., 1881, p. 148.
108 *Malbr. Manl.*, p. 358.

also endeavoured on all occasions to turn to their own account the perennial differences existing among the native powers.[109]

Though the European settlers made use of their native allies against each other, the procedure was reversed when the native chiefs were in want of money. At Malabar, in 1728, the Prince Regent being in great need of money and supplies, was at first refused by the English factors. He thereon applied to the Dutch, and offered them the Island of Dharmapattanam, where the English had a warehouse. As possession of the island was necessary to the conduct of the Tellicherry trade, the English were thus obliged to comply; but they secured in return, the monopoly of trade in Iruvalinad, Dharmapattanam and Randatarra, with permission to hoist their flag should their possession of these places be threatened by the Dutch or French.[110] The deed is dated 2nd November 1730, and is given below[111]:—

"Royal Writing to protect the trade of the English Company.

For the greater security of the English Company and their Trade in our Dominions, Be it known . . . . . That I, Ode Ormen, Prince Regent and Governor of the Palace of Palleé do promise free liberty to, and authorise the aforesaid English Company (and not to any other European nation whatsoever) for to trade and Traffick in . . . . . . our Dominions. I likewise promise them not to admit either the Dutch or French nation to make any Establishment or carry on any Trade in the country of Erbenadoo, Trentapatam nor Randa Tarra. That in case either the Dutch or French nation should hereafter pretend to Traffick or settle themselves in any of the aforesaid countrys, We do give full Liberty to the English Company to Hoist their Flag either on Trentapatam or Randoo Tarra . . . . "

The important resolution of the Supreme Council at Batavia to refuse further assistance to their native allies had an effect which might have been, but was not, foreseen—Dutch prestige declined. The foreigners were assisted from no benevolent motives, but only in anticipation of returns to be made when required. The refusal of assistance, left the native powers without inducement to assist the adventurers in any way.

In 1733 Calli-Quilon was threatened, and the Dutch Governor, A. Maten, was applied to. Some advice was offered, but aid was refused.[112]

In 1732–33 Malabar was invaded by the Canarese, and much disturbance caused to the trade of the English and Dutch. The Dutch commander at Cannanore, received orders from Cochin, to stop the food supplies of the invaders; they otherwise abstained from interference. They were afraid of the post of Kadalai—whose neutrality was essential to the continuance of their pepper trade on the Valarpattanam river—falling into the hands of the English. The latter had been drawn into hostilities, and desiring the co-operation of the Dutch, undertook to lay no claim to Kadalai should it be taken. The Dutch thereon joined their forces, on the understanding that Kadalai should be razed to the ground; and the Canarese were attacked and dispersed.[113]

Towards the end of 1736 the Dutch in Malabar, wished the Prince Regent to sell them 100 candies of pepper, at 13½ Venetians, to be drawn from any of his districts. He replied he had no concern with trade, and that he had assigned such privileges to the English, who only bought pepper with the free consent of the owners. The Dutch then threatened to refuse further assistance against the Canarese. The negotiations proceeded, and in the beginning of 1737 a nominal agreement was settled, whereby the Dutch should

---

109 *Malbr. Manl.*, pp. 72, 359–61.
110 *Malbr. Manl.*, p. 361.
111 *Malbr. Treaties* p. 18.
112 *Malbr. Manl.*, p. 393.
113 *Malbr. Manl.*, pp. 363, 366.

lend assistance on the condition of their receiving 1,000 candies of pepper at about half the ordinary market rates. This arrangement, though in violation of the English concession of 1730, did not disturb the English factors, who recorded that, though the Dutch performed their part, the Prince Regent would not do his. He could not have procured, without war, the produce of any of his districts at half market rates; and his avarice prevented his first paying the market price, and then selling at a loss to himself.[114]

In August of the same year the English offered the Prince Regent a consideration of Rs. 5,000 if he would refuse to deal with any other power; and on Rs. 1,000 being paid, it was ratified. Shortly after, the Dutch retired from Madakkara to Cochin, being unable to settle matters with the Canarese; and their agreement with the Prince Regent having led to nothing. Their trade at Cannanore had been reduced to small proportions, as the English, in possession of the Madakkara fort, were able to exclude them from the Valarpattanam river.[115]

In 1737 Protestant missions were started by Sartorius at Cuddalore, Sadras and Negapatam.[116]

In 1739 Van Imhoff became Governor on the West Coast. He saw that it was essential for their trade, to check the power of Travancore, under whose protection the English worked. He personally carried a protest against the Raja's occupation of territory acquired in 1734. The mission met with no success, and Van Imhoff threatened to invade Travancore. The Raja replied that doubtless the Dutch could do so, but he could retire into the forest. The Dutchman retorted that, where the Travancoreans could go, the Dutch could follow. The Raja then sarcastically observed that he had been thinking of invading Europe.

Unfortunately for the Dutch, their resources were but small, and the desultory war which followed led to little result.[117]

At the beginning of 1740 the French attempted a settlement at Chetwai, but the Zamorin was against it, and the Dutch forced them to retire.[118]

In consequence of the determination of the Dutch in 1721, to abstain from engaging themselves in wars, in support of their native allies, the Cochin Raja was put to sore straits. The Travancoreans, who had made a prisoner of D'Lanoy, at their siege of the Dutch fort of Colachel in 1741, with his aid raised a standing army. They thenceforth became masters of the country; and with them increased the prosperity of the English trade.[119]

In 1744 war broke out between England and France. In the complications which ensued, the English, in 1745, asked the Dutch for permission to make an attack on Cannanore; but it was refused. Owing to the great losses sustained by the French at sea, their commerce was carried in Dutch ships.[120]

When the French captured Madras in 1746, Fabricius the missionary in charge, retired to Pulicat.[121]

In 1747 some improvements were carried out by the English at Fort St. David, and numbers of houses were demolished. The Dutch factory was situated 700 yards north of the fort. The Dutch had left Cuddalore and Devanapatam for Porto Novo in 1745. The permission of the Dutch Governor at Negapatam was requested to the deserted factory being demolished. He declined, without reference to Batavia.[122]

---

114 *Malbr. Manl.*, p. 369.
115 *Malbr. Manl.*, pp. 371–72, *Malbr.* T. 28, 33.
116 *Mad. Manl. Admn.*, pp. 622, 624.
117 *Malbr. Manl.*, p. 393.
118 *Malbr. Manl.*, p. 375.
119 *Malbr. Manl.*, p. 351.
120 *Malbr. Manl.*, pp. 381–82.
121 *Mad. Manl. Admn.*, p. 622.
122 *S. Arcot Dt. Manl.*, pp. 63–64.

In a proclamation, dated 2nd May 1749, by the "President of and for all affairs of the Honourable United Company of Merchants of England trading to the East Indies on the Coast of India, Persia and Arabia, Governor and Commander-in-Chief of His Majesty's Castle and Island of Bombay and its dependencies." An alleged claim by the Dutch, to the exclusive trade in opium, is repudiated. It is stated that—

"Whereas the Dutch East India Company by the Chiefs of their respective Factories said to be by the authority of their General and Council at Batavia, did, in the year 1746, by notification affixed at their respective Factories, pretend to an exclusive right of Trade in opium, &c., as set forth in said notification. To the End therefore that those trading under the protection of the Honourable United English East India Company may not be discouraged from carrying on their lawful Trade and Commerce, they have thought proper in their Commands to their President and Council of Bombay, dated 17th of June last, not only utterly to deny such a right to belong to the Dutch East India Company, but in case any of their ships should be molested in carrying on their commerce, have empowered their said President and Council to give the Commanders of them positive orders to visit such hostilities and to make reprisals not only in defence of themselves but also of English country ships carrying their Pass and navigated by a British Commander. The said Honourable United English East India Company being resolved and determined to suffer no infringement in their Trade and Commerce and that every one may be apprized thereof, this Declaration is ordered to be affixed at their several Factories in the East Indies. . . . "[123]

In 1750 the Dutch erected the church now used by the English in Tuticorin.[124]

In the same year, ships of 900 tons could find accommodation in Masulipatam harbour. There was no other on the coast between it and Cape Comorin.[125]

The hostilities, which had been carried on between the Dutch and Travancoreans since 1739, came to an end in 1753. The treaty stipulated that the Dutch were to withdraw from engagements entered into with other Malabar princes, who might be attacked by the Travancore Raja. They were not to interfere in their disputes, afford shelter to the malcontents, or interefere with any of the enterprises entered into by the Travancore king. In return, they were to get 4 annas on every 25 lbs. of pepper supplied from Travancore, or from such territories as might be conquered by that State. After the treaty had been completed, and the Travancore frontier advanced as far as Cochin, the Raja repudiated it. He told the Dutch factors at Cochin, that they were no longer a power, but only petty merchants, and if they wanted pepper, they could go to the bazaars and purchase it at market rates. This they eventually had to do. The treaty gave the finishing stroke to Dutch influence in Malabar.[126]

The chief historical fact connected with Sadras, was a conference for the formation of a treaty between the French and English in 1754.[127]

In 1754 the fort of Mount Deli, once occupied by the Dutch as an outwork of Cannanore, was sold to the French by the Cherakal Raja.[128]

In 1755–56 the Zamorin attacked Chetwai, drove in the Dutch outposts, and took Cranganore, Paroor and Verapoly. The Travancore Raja also made an attack on the south, and took Tekkankur, Vadakkankur, Purakkat and other places.[129]

In 1755 the Bednur Raja laid an embargo on grain, and thus, for as long as it lasted, placed the Dutch at Cannanore in a state of comparative famine.[130]

When Madras was attacked by Labourdonnais in 1756, the Capuchin missionaries were ordered to quit the town and go to Pulicat. They remained there till the siege was raised three years later.[131]

---

[123] *Malbr. Treaties*, p. 100.
[124] *Tinly. Dt. Manl.*, pp. 60–61.
[125] *Mad. Manl. Admn.* p. 253.
[126] *Malbr. Manl.*, p. 393.
[127] *Chingpt. Dt. Manl.*, p. 90.
[128] M.J.L.S., 1879, p. 120.
[129] *Malbr. Manl.*, p. 403.
[130] *Malbr. Manl.*, p. 215.
[131] *Mad. Manl. Admn.*, p. 627.

Clive captured the Dutch settlement at Chinsurah near Calcutta in 1758.[132]

The Fort at Chetwai, which had been taken from the Dutch by the Zamorin in 1755–56, was recovered by them in 1758. A peace, disadvantageous to the Dutch, was concluded, whereby they obtained three islands off Palliport; but the other encroachments which had been made on their territories remained unchecked.[133]

The Dutch factory at Cuddalore, which the English proposed to remove in 1748, was demolished in 1758, and a house in Cuddalore was given to the Dutch in exchange.[134]

The fort of Sadras was surprised and taken by the French in 1758, but the Dutch regained it in 1759.[135]

In a grant of King Badacalamcur, Regent of Colastri, dated 9th September 1760, to the Honourable United English East India Company, the previous grants made to the English are confirmed. In the second article it is stated: "We now in order the more firmly to establish this privilege unto them, and especially to prevent the Dutch or any one else purchasing the pepper of Randatera, further consent to the company placing their people, both by land and sea, and in any part they may judge proper to frustrate it . . . ."[136]

In 1761 Muhammad Yusuf of Tinnevelly placed himself at the head of 4,000 sepoys and some cavalry, and marched against the Dutch.[137]

Hyder Ali is reported to have stated in 1766, that "the English were destined to be the masters of all India unless a change soon took place. They were already Masters of the whole of Bengal, of the Greatest part of the Coromandel coast, they are trying to get Malabar under them, and they have it in contemplation to send an expedition to China!" He was, he added, determined to prevent this coming to pass, and that he looked to the Dutch to aid him in expelling the English.

This conversation was repeated to H. Kroonenberg, the Dutch Chief at Cannanore, who, in his anxiety to show his sympathy, returned a visit of Hyder's in great state, mounted on the latter's elephant.

At Calicut, Dutch Commissioners met Hyder on his invasion of the province, and discussed a proposed alliance between them. The conference was without result, as the Dutch, to have accepted the terms, would have had to fight the English both at home and abroad. They were, moreover, too weak to have affected results, but were obliged to keep up an appearance of strength they did not possess.

Hyder made a demand from the Travancore Raja, who, trusting to the help of the English, made a negative reply. On the demand being repeated, the reply was an advancement of the Travancore lines to within range of the Dutch fort at Cranganore. In their fear of Hyder Ali, the Dutch required the Travancoreans to refrain from work within Dutch limits.

Hyder Ali demanded that four lakhs of rupees, and eight elephants should be supplied by the Cochin Raja. The Dutch interceded, and the payment finally made by their ally of Cochin was two lakhs of rupees and three elephants.[138]

A mission was sent from Madras to Kandy "in conseqence of application made to you by the Emperor of Ceylon solliciting our assistance against his Enemies the Dutch."[139] It was stated, that the behaviour of people about the court, was very ceremonious, with many professions of friendship, but with little sincerity. They were great proficients in

---

132 *Mad. Manl. Admn.*, p. 2.
133 *Malbr. Manl.*, p. 403.
134 *S. Arcot Dt. Manl.*, pp. 63, 64.
135 *Chingpt. Dt. Manl.*, pp. 177–182.
136 *Malbr. T.* p. 63.
137 *Mdu. Cty.* p. 281.
138 *Malbr. Manl.*, pp. 409, 411.
139 *Mily. Sundry book*, No. 17. Mr. Pybus' mission to Kandy, 1762.

dissimulation, and not to be confided in. The king himself entertained an implacable enmity against the Dutch, and would almost submit to any terms to induce the English to assist in driving them off the island; but the Dutch had a powerful interest behind them.

Among other particulars, it is stated, that "the trade carried on by the Dutch in elephants is one which yielded very considerable profit. The king reserved to himself the right of catching these animals, and the Dutch were obliged to annually apply, as a matter of form, for permission to do so. This was always granted under a restriction not to exceed in number, usually between twenty and thirty. Little regard is however paid to it, and I am informed, that at Matura, Colombo and Jaffnapatam, where these animals only are hunted for, the Dutch do not catch less than 150 and sometimes 200 in one year." Those who caught and tamed the elephants were paid at the rate of 50 dollars for animals with teeth and 25 for those without them.

Records of the period, refer to charges made against a Dutch Governor, of assisting the English in their previous mission to Kandy.

"Proceedings of the President and Council of Fort St. George in their Military Department regarding the Demand made by the Governor and Council of Negapatam for the Delivery up of Christian Van Teylingen, Esq., late Governor of that place.

May 30th.

"Anchord in this road about Noon a Dutch Ship with a Pendant called the Rotterdam and saluted the Fort, which was returned—about 2 o'clock. Three Gentlemen disembarked being saluted with 15 Guns from the ship and on their landing the like compliment was paid them finding by a Note from the ship they were Mr. Van Teylingen, late Governor of Negapatam, the Captain and a Writer."

After Mr. Van Teylingen had been ashore, he requested that some boats might be sent to take off his baggage. But meanwhile a 'Dutch Snow' came into the roads and landed a party of soldiers on board the *Rotterdam*, and when the boats approached, threatened to fire on them. In the evening, a party landed from the 'Snow' and delivered a letter, to the effect that Christian Van Teylingen had deserted his post of Governor, without making a formal transport, and that as he might visit Madras, it was requested that he might not be granted protection.

Mr. Christian Van Teylingen protested, and his goods were ultimately delivered to him. The Council held a consultation, and sent a letter of protest to the Governor and Council of Negapatam, wherein it was stated " . . . . We cannot sufficiently express our surprize at the Behaviour of the persons sent after him (Mr. Van Teylingen) in a Dutch Snow which came into the road without shewing any colours till she came to an anchor, tho' those of the Fort had been flying from her first appearance, and immediately after sent a party of armed soldiers on Board the ship *Rotterdam*, and forcibly and unwarrantably seized all the papers and effects of Mr. Van Teylingen, without making any application to Us, or giving us the least intimation of their business, which is an act so contrary to the Laws of Nations, disrespectful to the British Flag and such an Insult to our Government, that we are under the necessity of protesting against you and all others concerned therein for all consequences that may arise therefrom, our Protest accordingly comes endorsed . . . . ."

The effects were ordered to be "deposited in a Godown under the charge of the Secretary till we know what Demands the Governor and Council of Negapatam may have on him. In the meantime the Secretary is directed to deliver to him such wearing apparel and other personal Necessaries as He may want immediately for his own use."

A great mass of consultations and correspondence, extending up to September 1765, followed, in which the Dutch preferred some charges of robbery against Van Teylingen and wanted possession of his person, which however the English refused. In a letter from Christian Van Teylingen to the Governor of Fort St. George, is an extract from a letter, sent to the former by the General of Batavia, which explains why the Dutch were so eager for his capture. "The Discontent the Superior Council found upon account of the incomprehensible assistance to the English in their way to Tondy likewise 3 Foreigners by our Company's Ship, you'll find by the General Letter, and I in particular must acknowledge in regard to the first article my great Surprize of your imprudent and never heard of step and which must certainly occasion be very prejudicial to our nation in regard to yourself, and our Interest must have certainly led you another way, for it is impossible for me to conceive for what reason and with what intention you was seduced, for I must say Seduced, for else it was impossible that you could directly contrary to our Intention favour the English in such a point, and to our considerable Prejudice, for how is it possible that to this pernicious and dangerous competitor in our Trade upon the coast you could show the way to such a place where our affairs on the Madura Coast is in danger and quite put to the Ballance in one way or another."

Another extract from a letter from a "Gentleman of the Superior Council" stated, that the principal indictment was "your assisting the English with Thonys and Chilangues to Tondy in an affair which appear'd to the Regency of great and dangerous consequences." A number of others of similar import follow.[140]

In 1766 the Dutch concluded a treaty with the Native powers in Ceylon, agreeing to pay a certain yearly tribute.[141]

The Tinnevelly mission was originally an outstation of Tranquebar. In 1771 a Dutch Christian went to reside and carry on mission work at Palamcottah.[142]

In 1771 the Dutch hold on the country was still on the decline, and their policy of reducing the number of forts, was carried out by the sale to Ali Raja, of Fort St. Angelo at Cannanore. Those at Chetwai and Cranganore were considerably reduced, and that at Cochin had been allowed to become so ruinous, that Commander Moens had to take steps to repair it.[143]

In September 1773 the Fort of Tanjore was taken by the English, and handed over to the Navab Muhammad Ali. Shortly after, the Navab requested the English to assist him in recovering from the Dutch Company, districts which he had assigned to them, in return for money borrowed to meet the expenses of some recent expeditions against him. These districts extended twelve miles inland from Negapatam, and included the nine Maghanams of Kivalur, Sikkal, Tevur, Sembiyamahadevi, Palakkurchi, Maghilai, Killugudi, Adiyakkamangalam and Tiruppundi valued at 3,84,000 pagodas. There were also included, the two seaports of Nagur and Topputurai of the value of 75,000 pagodas. The price settled, was 4,59,400 pagodas, to which was added a lump payment of 59,545 pagodas, in commutation of the annual tribute of 5,000 chakrams and three elephants paid by the Dutch. This made a total of 5,18,945 pagodas, for which the Dutch took bonds; but only paid 4,84,545 pagodas. They also had possession of jewels worth five lakhs of pagodas, in trust for money they had advanced two years previously. Nagur was taken

[140] *Mily. Sundry Records*, 1765, No. 30.
[141] *Mad. Manl. Admn.*, p. 32.
[142] *Mad. Manl. Admn.*, p. 625.
[143] *Malbr. Manl.*, p. 421.

possession of, by an English detachment, and the money which had been paid by the Dutch was returned to them.[144]

Hyder Ali, in his invasion of the west coast in 1776, demanded of the Dutch at Cochin, permission to pass through their territories into Travancore. The Dutch fort at Cranganore, covered the west flank of the Travancore frontier. Passage was refused, as a reference had to be made to Batavia. The same demand had been made, and a similar reply given ten years before. As the Dutch had had all that time to consider the matter, Hyder regarded the answer as evasive, and threatened to annihilate them. His troops thereafter invaded Cochin, and received a tribute. The Dutch thought the matter was ended, but they soon after received a letter from Sirdar Khan, demanding the surrender of Chetwai, on the ground that it had formed a part of the Zamorin's territory, which they had taken from him; and that they had promised its return within a certain period. That time had now expired, and as Hyder was, by conquest, the Zamorin's successor, he demanded possession. The Dutch refused to hand over the place, and Sirdar Khan took possession of the custom-house, and made further threats of attack. He stated, that Hyder had been insulted by the evasive reply of the Dutch Governor, but that he had no desire to proceed to hostilities, and asked passage for the troops to Travancore. Governor Moens replied, he was glad they wished to be friendly, but he wished they would leave his territory, and not allow troops to approach Cranganore fort. An unsuccessful attempt to surprise the fort had, in the meantime, been made; and the Sirdar demanded twenty years' accounts of the lands of Paponetty, and the territory which the Dutch had received from the Zamorin in 1758.

The Dutch saw that a conflict was being forced on them; but as they had only 200 soldiers, they strengthened their forts, and endeavoured to gain the co-operation of the Native powers. Travancore declined, and urgent appeals for reinforcements were sent to Ceylon. Some troops arrived, and the Mysoreans retired. A force of 180 men was sent from Cochin, in the ship *Hoolwerf*, to pursue them, but they fell into an ambush on landing, and Chetwai had to surrender. The Dutch captives were sent in chains to Seringapatam, where they took service under Hyder Ali.[145]

In 1776–77 the export returns of the Dutch Company on the east coast, were placed at 4,27,131 francs; but the charges amounted to 4,52,133 francs. At that time, their possessions were divided into seven governments. The seventh government included the Coromandel coast, with Negapatam as the capital. Under it, were the factories at Sadras, Bimlipatam, Palkole and Jaganaikpore (Jaganadhapuram). The last named—a portion of Cocanada on the south of the river—was originally known as Daatijeroon. The factory was defended by earthen ramparts, and had two other villages subordinate to it. There, bleaching of calicoes and other piece-goods was carried on.[146]

The Dutch in Europe, were jealous of subject liberty, yet they granted their Indian officials almost sovereign powers, which it was considered necessary they should possess, in order to secure the respect of the Native powers, who were, and still are, extremely observant of the prestige of those foreigners whose lot it is to be cast among them. Though unassuming in private life, the officials were very tenacious of the rank they held. The Governor-General at Batavia, and the subordinate Indian Governors, were obliged to appear in public with regal pomp and magnificence. In this respect, considering their

---

[144] *Tanj. Dt. Manl.*, pp. 803, 809. [145] *Malbr. Manl.*, pp. 422, 424; M.J.L.S., 1879, p. 116. [146] *God. Dt. Manl.*, p. 196.

position and object, they acted wisely; but it was carried to so great an extent, that it led to the absorbing of all their profits, and contributed to their downfall.[147]

In this connection, an account of the ceremony observed at the house of the Governor-General at Batavia is interesting:—

"The Governor-General receives his guests sitting at the step at the door, dressed in a black waist-coat, with a stiff linen cap on; and, when they have all come, the General says: 'Friends, pull off your coats'; upon which every one takes off his coat, hat and sword. They then sit down on chairs placed in a row on the step, every one according to his rank; and if it should happen that any one does not observe this, he is told by the General: 'That is not your place, you must sit there.' Every one has then a glass of beer, and the toast is 'A pleasant evening to you'; after that a pipe of tobacco, and then the conversation begins, but in such a manner that each speaks to his neighbour without daring to speak so loud that the supreme commander may hear, who only converses for that evening with the person who sits next him, and who is, consequently, the highest in rank; and all that the General says aloud is 'The ladies' health.' As soon as he has said this, every one jumps from his seat with a glass of wine which he had already in his hand, forming all together a large half circle, and, with their heads bent forward, they call out 'The General's lady's health'; then follow the healths of every person present, each rising and bowing when his health is drunk. This ceremony is prolonged by the General till the clock strikes nine, when every one receives his hat, coat and sword again, and obliging himself to drink to the General's health, who receives it with 'Thank ye for my health.' Every one then takes his leave."[148]

In February 1777 the Commandant and Resident of Chetwai returned from Seringapatam to Cochin, and informed Governor Adrian Van Moens, that the prisoners, made at the surrender of Chetwai, had been released; that Hyder Ali disowned the acts of his commander Sirdar Khan. He had expressed a friendly feeling for the Dutch, and wished to enter into treaty with them. The Governor evaded, without declining the proposals.[149]

In the beginning of 1777 a letter arrived in Cochin from the Council at Batavia, being an answer to the reference on the demands of Hyder Ali made during the previous year. It was sent to Hyder's camp, accompanied by a missive and presents from the Governor of Cochin. In 1778 the commandant strengthened the Cochin fort with seven bastions and ditches, and determined to take the offensive in an endeavour to recover lost territory.[150] The Cranganore Raja's palace was first stormed and taken. The Dutch then proceeded to Bellapattoo and Chetwai. They made an unsuccessful attack on the latter fort, and retired with some loss. They endeavoured to get the assistance of the Travancoreans, but did not succeed.

Hyder Ali was indignant at their proceedings; but, being engaged in war with the English, he contented himself by sacking the Dutch factory at Porto Novo, and capturing the Resident.[151]

In 1779 a tidal wave swept over Masulipatam, and the sea flowed twelve feet deep in the Dutch factory. Goods to the value of 80,000 pagodas were destroyed.[152]

In 1781 war broke out between the English and Dutch, and the Coromandel settlements of the latter succumbed. These included Sadras,[153] Bimlipatam,[154] Jaganadhapuram,[155] Policole,[156] Porto Novo,[157] Tuticorin[158] with its nine subordinate commercial

---

[147] *Essay on the East India Trade*, 1770, p. 9; *God. Dt. Manl.*, p. 200.

[148] *View of the Present State of the Dutch Settlements in the East Indies, London*, 1780, p. 5; *God. Dt. Manl.*, pp. 200–1.

[149] *Malbr. Manl.*, p. 425.

[150] *Malbr. Manl.*, vol. ii. p. ccccxx.

[151] *Malbr. Manl.*, p. 426.

[152] *Kist. Dist. Manl.*, p. 98.

[153] *Chingpt. District.*

[154] *Vizag. District.*

[155] Suburb of Cocanada, the chief town of the Gódávari District. Here they had a factory with the dependent villages of Gollapalem, and land at Gundavaram.

[156] Six miles from Narsapur in the Gódávari District, with dependent village of Kontera.

[157] *S. Arcot District.*

[158] *Tnvlly. District.*

factories, Alwar Tinnevelly, Koilpabam, Shaindmangalam, Munnapur, Peramkoil, Island of Alandale, Island of Freshwater, Kilkarai (in the Madura district), Cape Comorin, Sadras, Pulicat,[159] with its fort, factory and dependencies consisting of Irakam Island, and villages of Vanjivakam, Ararivakam, and Kanavandurai; Negapatam.[160]

In 1781 during Hyder Ali's attack on Tellicherry, the store of gunpowder in the garrison ran short, and one of the Factors went to Cochin by sea, to get a supply. Shortly after, on the 27th August, news of the war between England and Holland was received. The Factor was, in consequence, detained as a prisoner of war, and his effects seized. He was later, released in November, in exchange for a relative of Governor Van Anglebeck.[161]

In 1782 Tuticorin fell to the English.[162]

After the reduction of the Coromandel settlements, preparations were made for taking those in Ceylon. In 1782 an Agent was sent from Madras, to gain the consent of the King of Kandy, whereby he was to provide supplies for the English force, and send another to co-operate with it. The king however would only confer with an ambassador direct from England.[163]

Trincomalee was captured by the English in 1782, but restored to the Dutch the following year.[164]

In 1783 the Dutch recovered Chetwai from Tippu Sultan. During the next year however orders arrived from Batavia that it was to be returned to him.[165]

The poligars of Tinnevelly, in their wars against the English, were frequently assisted by the Dutch. In 1783 some of them, encouraged by the latter, rebelled, and an expedition was despatched against them. The fort of Panjalamkurichi was taken; and in it were found the original treaty with the Dutch, and 40,000 star pagodas.[166]

On the 20th May 1784, peace was signed between England and the States-General of the United Provinces, providing for a mutual restitution of the places captured during the late war. Negapatam was an exception, it being provided that it would be restored "in case the States should ever have an equivalent to offer." It has since remained an English possession.[167]

Among the places thus restored in 1785, in accordance with the above treaty, were Bimlipatam, Jaganadhapuram, Palkole, Porto Novo factory, Pulicat, Sadras and Tuticorin.[168]

The Dutch factories in the Gódávari district paid a quit-rent to the English East India Company.

In 1787 it was ascertained, that at the Dutch factory in Palkole, previous to the war lately terminated, there had annually been provided, 400 bales of white long cloth, of from 12 to 14 punjams for the European market, and quantities of chintz and other dyed goods for the Indian Archipelago.[169]

At the factory of Jaganadhapuram, with its dependent villages of Gollapalem and Gundavaram, there had annually been imported spice to the value of about a lakh of

---

159 *Chingpt. District.*

160 *Mad. Manl. Admn.*, pp. 2, 183, 186; M.J.L.S., 1879, pp. 104, 125, 126; and 1881, pp. 104–5.; *Lists of Antiq.*, pp. 14, 41, 173, 189; *Chingpt. Dt. Manl.*, pp. 19, 76.

161 *Malbr. Manl.*, p. 432.

162 *Tnvlly. Dt. Manl.*, p. 45; *Lists of Antiq.*, p. 308.

163 *Mad. Manl. Admn.*, p. 32.

164 *Mad. Manl. Admn.*, p. 118

165 *Malbr. Manl.*, p. 426.

166 *Tnvlly. Dt. Manl.*, pp. 45, 54.

167 M.J.L.S., 1879, p. 126.

168 M. J. L. S., 1879, pp. 104, 125; *Lists of Antiq.*, p. 308; *Tnvlly. Dt. Manl.*, p. 45.

169 *God. Dt. Manl.*, p. 203.

Madras pagodas; one half was in gold and the other in copper and spices. Of this sum, forty thousand pagodas were expended in the purchase of chay-dyed goods, and six thousand for white long cloth at this factory and that at Palkole.

Private traders also exported to Batavia and the East, coarse punjam cloth, and fine long cloth of values up to twenty pagodas the piece.

It had been the custom at these villages, to charge import and export duties of 5 and 3 per cent. in the Cocanada river. The 'Committee of Circuit on Zemindaries,' in their report at this time, stated, they were unable to ascertain the grounds on which the Dutch made these claims, as they only occupied one side of the river.[170] Among minor disputes between the English and Dutch, after the former had gained the sovereignty, the following incident is quoted. In 1788, the Collector of Mogalturru reported to Masulipatam, that the Renter of customs in Attili and Atsanta had complained of his having been interfered with by the Dutch at Palkole. Messrs. Van Haefton and Vanguel Diton, the Dutch officials, on hearing of the complaint, arrested the Renter's gumasta and sent him in charge of four peons to the Collector. In a letter, they stated that the Renter had, by his gumasta, attempted to stop the market at their town by threatening the people. They asked that he be punished in order "that he might never undertake more such and other like brutalities under our flag and colours." The Collector thought the matter had political significance, and that the Dutch were attempting an increase of power, or an alteration of the terms under which they held their villages. It was, however, merely a matter of minor importance: one party was indignant at the closing of the market; the other at the arrest of his assistant.[171]

A church was built by the Dutch during their occupation of Tangasseri in 1789.[172]

During June–September 1788 Tippu Sultan menaced the subjugation of Travancore, and made an ineffectual attempt at alliance with the Dutch. In 1789 he offered to purchase the forts of Cochin, Cranganore and Ayacotta. The Dutch did not close with his offer, but consulted with Travancore how to avoid the Mysoreans, or else draw the English into the struggle, should they themselves be unable to keep clear of it. As a means to this end, the forts of Cranganore and Ayacotta were sold to Travancore under the conditions stated in the following deed :—

"The Illustrious and Mighty King of Travancore Wanjie Walla Martanda Rama Warmer, having sent his First State Minister and Dalava, His Excellency Krishna Poola, to the Honourable, &c., &c., John Gerard Van Anglebeck, Councellor in Ordinary of Netherlands India, and Governor of the Forts and Possessions of the Illustrious and mighty Netherlands East India Company on the coast of Malabar, to purchase from the said Company and receive over the fort of Cranganore and the outpost of Ayacotta with the plantations and fields belonging thereto: and they, having agreed on the terms, have concluded the sale on the following conditions :—

"The Dalawa Krishna Poolah, has for his master bought, and Governor Van Anglebeck has on account of the Company sold to the King of Travancore for the sum of three hundred thousand Surat silver rupees the Fort of Cranganore and the outpost of Ayacottah; with the cannon and thereto belonging ammunition as they at present are, as also the powder, but no firelocks, cartridges or other articles and moreover the following plantations and gardens :—

	RS.
"The Musquito Island rented to Bellote Duzepo Pailo for	300
"The garden of Kilo Barky rented for	115
" Do. of Ascentio de Roza rented for	190

[170] *God. Dt. Manl.*, p. 203.
[171] *God. Dt. Manl.*, p. 204.
[172] *Malbr. Manl.*, vol. ii., p. ccccxxii.

		RS.
"The garden	of Naga Shetty rented for	164
Do.	of Hendrick Meyer rented for	230
Do.	of Bappoo Probu rented for	64
Do.	of Allewyn rented for	310
Do.	of Dama Moossa rented for	1,220
Do.	of Arkell Ittopœ rented for	119
Do.	of Konotœ Barky rented for	115

"The purchase and sale is concluded with this condition that the King of Travancore shall not prevent the passage past the fort, either to boats belonging to the Company, or to the King of Cochin and his subjects, but all the same should they be empty or laden with rice, paddy or goods of any denomination whatever, as also rafts of wood and bamboos, &c., &c., in a word all goods whatever without exception are to be allowed free, without molestation to pass and repass, and no new duties to be charged thereon.

"The king promises expressly that the firewood, which must be brought from above Cranganore, shall not be prevented on any pretext whatever, and no new charges laid thereon, but the contrary will assist the forwarding the same to Cochin.

"The Lepers' House at Palliport with its adjoining buildings, gardens and other grounds belonging thereto, is to remain in the Company's full and free possession.

"The Roman Churches at Cranganore and Ayacottah having for a long time been under the Company are to remain so, and the King is not to trouble himself with them or the Priests; the Christians are to remain vassals of the Company and must not be burthened with any new taxes.

"The Priests' house at Palliport, which the Governor built and made present to the church, is to remain to the churches and no new tax laid thereon.

"The inhabitants retain their houses, gardens and plantations, which are now in their possession and as long as they remain Christians are like other Roman Catholic vassals of the Company, and must not therefore on any pretext whatever have any new taxes laid on them, but they are to be held answerable to pay unto the King whatever they formerly paid to the Company.

"The King promises to pay the sum of fifty thousand Rupees ready money, before the delivering over the above-mentioned forts and ground and the remainder being two hundred and fifty thousand Rupees to be paid in the four next following years at equal period and to be carried to the credit side of the pepper account yearly, to the amount of sixty-two thousand five hundred Rupees, for the fulfilling of which the merchants David Rahaboy, Ephrain Cohen and Anta Setty bind themselves as bondsmen or legal debtors.

"All this agreed to in the city of Cochin in the year Koilang 974 the 19th of the month Karkadagom or the 31st July 1789.

(Signed) J. G. ANGLEBACK.

(A true copy.)

(Signed) J. A. GRANT,
Sub-Secretary."

In regard to the transaction, the English Company instructed that, if the places belonged to Cochin before it became tributary to Mysore, the sale would be upheld; but if not, Travancore would require to restore them.

The purchase of the two forts from the Dutch, precipitated the attack on Travancore by Tippu, and involved him in war with the English, which terminated with the cession of Malabar in 1792.[173]

---

173 *Malbr. Manl.*, pp. 134, 458-60; *Malbr. T.*, pp. 132–34.

Chetwai was taken by the English from Tippu Sultan in 1790.[174]

In 1790 the authorities at Cochin passed a resolution, that the English factory at Anjengo should be destroyed.[175]

In a treaty between the Honourable United East India Company and the Raja of Cochin, dated 6th January 1791, article the sixth states :—" That in consideration of a Treaty, which subsists between the Honorable Dutch East India Company, and the Raja Rama Warma of Cochin, the Honourable Governor in Council of Madras, not wishing to enter into any condition which may not be compatible with the spirit of the Treaty subsisting between the above-mentioned parties, it is agreed that Raja Warma shall become tributary to the Honourable English East India Company only for those districts, and place before recited, which were in the possession of Tippoo Sultan, and for which the said Raja paid him tribute, and with which the Honourable Dutch Company have no concern."

The English Company had rented Chetwai to the Raja of Cochin, but were uncertain as to whether their action might not lead to disputes with the Dutch Company. Van Anglebeck, Governor of Cochin, had been asked to state what engagements existed between his Company and Cochin, but had refused. This clause had therefore been inserted.[176]

Malabar was ceded by treaty to the English in 1792.[177]

In 1794 the Dutch factories at Palkole and Jaganadhapuram, subordinate to the English at Masulipatam, were asked for payment of two years' tribute. For the former, 286 pagodas, and for the latter 434 pagodas were due. The first was paid, but for the other, exemption was claimed, on the plea that the Netherlands Company had abandoned all commerce on the coast for the past two years.[178]

On the 1st February, war was declared by France against England and Holland. In February 1795, after the proclamation of the Batavian Republic, of alliance with France, the Stadtholder, who had fled to England, addressed a circular to all the Dutch Colonial Governors to admit British troops into all the "Settlements, Plantations, Colonies and Factories in the East Indies" to prevent their falling to the French.[179]

The Dutch factories on the east and west coasts fell to the English in 1795. Bimlipatam, Sadras, Jaganadhapuram, Palkole, Porto Novo factory, Pulicat and Tuticorin surrendered.[180]

The records of the year, give the papers relating to the capitulation of Pulicat.

To Mr. Macleod, returning the articles of capitulation for the surrender of Pulicat and its Dependencies, with the final Resolutions of this Government annexed to each Article.

"The articles of capitulation proposed by the Government of Pulicat I have received, and this Government having bestowed upon them the most deliberate consideration, I now return them to you with the Resolutions which have been passed upon each article, expressed in an opposite column. In communicating them to the Dutch Government, it will be necessary that they should be made explicitly to understand that they are final, and that I expect an immediate acquiescence to the capitulation as it now stands.

FORT ST. GEORGE,
17th July 1795.

I am, &c., &c.,
(Signed) HOBART."

---

[174] *Malbr. Manl.*, pp. 496, 666. [175] *Malbr. Manl.*, p. 421. [176] *Malbr. T.*, p. 90.
[177] *Malbr. Manl.*, p. 476. [178] *God. Dt. Manl.*, p. 203. [179] *Malbr. Manl.*, pp. 498, 506
[180] M.J.L.S., 1879, pp. 104, 125 ; *Tnvlly. Dt. Manl.*, p. 45 ; *Lists of Antiq.*, p. 308.

Received the following letters :—

"The President lays before the Board the following articles of capitulation for the surrender of Pulicat transmitted to his Lordship by Mr. Macleod :—

Articles of capitulation for the surrender of Pulicat and its dependencies to his Britanick Majesty.

Articles of capitulation by the under-written Governor and Council, on the part of the General Netherlands East India Company, on account of their inability to defend their possessions, on the summons made by the Right Honorable Lord Hobart, Governor and President of Fort St. George, according to the Resolution of the 10th and 16th instant, proposed to the Right Honorable Lord Hobart, Governor in Council at Fort St. George by which it is agreed to deliver over Pulicat and its dependencies to the Power and authority of his Britanick Majesty.

Article 1st.

Approved.

That an exact Inventory of all Public Property in Fort Geldria at Pulicat, as it stands on the 15th instant, shall be delivered to the British Commissary, and the said Public Property delivered over, according to the above Inventory, to the gentleman Appointed by the Government of Madras to receive it. The said Gentleman granting his Receipt for the same.

Article 2nd.

Approved.

That all Books, Charters, Letters, and other Papers belonging to the Honorable Dutch East India Company shall, as a Holy depositum, not be removed from Pulicat but carefully Kept distinct in the different departments to which they belong in the charge of the present Chiefs or Heads of those departments for the reasons mentioned in the following article.

Article 3rd.

Agreed that attested copies of such Books, &c., be sent to Europe and Batavia, but that the originals remain at Pulicat subject to the Inspection of the Government of Fort St. George.

As there is much arrear of business in the offices, especially in that of Trade and in the Pay books of this Head factory, since the year 1792–93, and the Gentlemen of the Dutch service shall be allowed to bring up that arrear to the present day, and it is requested, as an indulgence to our Governor, that he may send the annual Books, Statements, &c., to Europe and Batavia as opportunities may occur.

Article 4th.

Agreed.

The Garrison, which consists of 75 sepoys, as also their Native officers, are not to be Prisoners of War, but may be dismissed and permitted to deliver over their arms and accoutrements to their Commanding officer who will deliver the same to the British Commissary.

Article 5th.

Leave will be granted, unless under particular circumstances, by the Government of Madras, to the Dutch Company's servants, and free Merchants, to go to Europe or elsewhere, but any allowances by way of subsistence must cease; from the period of that Permission being granted.

The Governor and Council of Pulicat wishes to be favored with an Explanation whether the Dutch company's Servants, who, by the present arrangement, are deprived of their Employs, and other private Gentlemen, such as free Merchants, &c., under their Jurisdiction, tho' not in the service, are to be considered as free subjects of the States-General, and at liberty to go elsewhere, even to Europe, if they please, or is it expected they should apply to the Government of Madras for that Purpose. It is proposed also that, on account of the Governor Council and other Servants of the Dutch Company being deprived of their pay and Emoluments a subsistence shall be granted to them.

Article 6th.

Approved.

That all the said Company's servants, subjects, and other Inhabitants of Pulicat, and its subordinate companys factories, Natives as well as European shall retain the Right of Possession of their Private Property, of every description, without being molested in any manner whatever.

Article 7th.

Whatever may be done upon this Article must be, a subject for future consideration. It cannot be admitted as a part of the capitulation.

That all the said servants and others under the Government of Pulicat shall be granted permission to trade on equal terms and enjoy the same Immunities as his Brittanick Majesty's subjects in India.

Article 8th.

Agreed—but liable to the control of Government.

The cash belonging to the orphans, and that which the vestry has charge of, for the consistory, being money collected by Private Charity, shall, of course, be considered as Private Property, and shall remain under the administration of those to whom they have been entrusted.

Article 9th.

When the Information is given, Government will determine.

The above consistorial Fund having been found insufficient to maintain the Widows, and other indigent persons, proper objects of that charity, The Dutch Company have, ever since the 1st January last, contributed to their support Pagodas 37½ per month, the objects of the above charitable donation are strongly recommended to the Humanity of the British Government, proper Information will be given of the particulars of the situation of those poor people.

Article 10th.

Approved.

The exercise of divine service, such as has hitherto prevailed in the Dutch, Portuguese, and Malabar churches, shall be permitted to be performed in the usual places.

Article 11th.

Until the Kings pleasure be known.

That all civil causes shall be decided according to the Dutch Laws, and Regulations of the Dutch Company by the same Gentlemen who now compose the Court of Civil Judicature.

Article 12th.

Approved.

The Vendumaster, Curator adlites,* and Sequestrator,† do keep their Right to summon before the above Court and proceed, as by law directed, against all who are deficient in paying the cash belonging to their respective Departments, and the said Court shall have every protection and support from the British Government, in the exercise of their lawful functions.

Article 13th.

Approved.

The Secretary of the Political Department, as also his deputy, in the capacity of sworn clerk and Secretary of the above Court, should be continued in the Exercise of his office of Notary and that the same be granted to the Secretaries, or other authorized persons on the subordinate factories.

Article 14th.

Approved.

The publick Notarial deeds already entered, registered or passed by the above mentioned officer in behalf of Individuals, for their safety and security should remain as Secret documents that officers are trusted with, and of which deeds no person may require an Inspection or copy, except in cases in which the Sovereign or Magistrates are concerned. whose commands, as well as those of the above Civil Court, the Notary is to obey.

---

* That is administrator to the Estates of such Company's servants as die intestate.

† That is the person with whom sums in dispute are deposited, and who administers to those who die insolvent.

Article 15th.

Unnecessary and inadmissible.

The Company's Interpreter named Maudelelum Vencatachellum Naiq, Bramin named Coupiah, and merchants not subject to any other Jurisdiction but that of the Dutch Company, consequently not amendable to the Nabob's court or to that of his Dewan, should be entitled to the Privileges mentioned in the Articles 6th and 7th, and the two former do keep their usual Wages, or shall receive a subsistence, as serving both for the Affairs of the Dherbar and for the Explanation of the Dutch Company's Rights and Privileges, the custom and usages at Pulicat, in case any dispute should happen about them with the Nabob's Dewan here.

Article 16th.

This will be a subject of arrangement between the British Government and the Nabob of the Carnatic.

The duties of Pulicat collected by the Nabob, of which the Dutch Company are entitled to a share, are not paid up by him to a later date than the 31st August 1794, therefore this Arrear and what is further to be collected, shall be duly paid to the British Commissary.

Article 17th.

The suggestion will be attended to, but cannot be admitted as an article of the Capitulation.

The Company's villages Erikan Manguvauk and Aurewauk, as also the pieces of ground named Ranatoray, being Publickly rented once every three years were, on the 1st September 1794, rented to Magadalla Ramayah for the sum of 785 Star Pagodas per annum, for which amount he is to be yearly responsible; and it is proposed that the above farm given on the faith of the Dutch Company, should be continued to the said Renter, He paying his Rent to the British Government.

Article 18th.

Agreed.

To the Chiefs of Dutch Company's factories on the coast of Coromandel shall be sent a copy of these articles, and they shall be directed to draw out their capitulation and deliver over their factories, &c., on the terms herein stipulated.

Article 19th.

Agreed.

And to prevent all misunderstanding, and to insure the punctual performance of these conditions, the above articles be written twice in Dutch, and twice in English, and signed by and delivered to the contracting parties on both sides.

PULICAT, *the 16th July 1795.*

(Signed)	HOBART.	(Signed)	JACOB EILBRACHT.
(„)	EDWD. SAUNDERS.	(„)	FK. WM. BLOEME.
(„)	E. W. FALLOFIELD.	(„)	HM. HASZ.
		(„)	I. HANTER VISSCHER.

(A true copy.)

(Signed) DANL. INCE,
Deputy Secretary.

Counterparts of the articles of capitulation to be interchanged with the Government of Pulicat.

Ordered that the articles, with the observations thereon, be now signed, and that one copy in English and Dutch be retained in the office, and the other transmitted to Mr. Macleod at Pulicat. . . . . ."[181]

In July of the same year, an English force was sent against Cochin. The Governor M. Vanspall had provisioned the fort in anticipation of a siege. On the demand to surrender, the Governor at first refused, then agreed, and finally again refused. An attack was then begun, but the garrison shortly surrendered. The terms of capitulation

[181] *Mily. Records*, July 1795, p. 1982, *et seq.*

are contained in the following articles. Those of the Dutch are written in French, and signed by the Commandant J. L. Vanspall, and his Council, Decan, J. A. Cellarius, J. A. Schudz, Arnold Lunel and C. Vanspall. The answers of the English are written in that language, and signed by Major G. Petrie, Commander of the attacking force.

In the preliminary article, the Dutch proposed to deliver up the place on the 20th of the month, and requested that hostilities might cease.

The reply stated that they should be prisoners of war, that the fort should be delivered up to-morrow at noon, at which time detachments would be ordered to take possession of the western and Muttoncherry gates :—

" *Article 1st.**

Requested that the officers and military of the Garrison, who had defended Cochin, should march out of the New Port (Niew Poort) with the ordinary honours of war, with their arms and baggage, colours flying and drums beating, the match burning, and two pieces of cannon with their accoutrements.

Replied that the garrison shall march out as requested, and deposit their arms upon the esplanade, after which they must return prisoners of war.

Article 2nd.

All officers and soldiers will be taken in the easiest manner at English cost by their vessels to Batavia or Ceylon.

Inadmissible. They were to be disposed of as directed by the Commander-in-Chief.

" *Article 3 me.*

" Les officiers et soldats susdits prendrons avec eux leurs effets sans étre visités, leurs serviteurs, et esclaves, et ceux qui sont mariés auront la liberté de prendre leurs familles avex eux."

(The officers and soldiers aforesaid will take with them their effects without being searched, their servants, and slaves, and those who are married will have the liberty of taking their families with them.)

Granted, except with regard to slaves. It is a name unknown in a British Country.

Article 4th.

The Commandant, the Members of Council, the Police and officers of Police and commerce, the Ecclesiastical Council, the Militia, the Marine and other servants drawing pension, and who are in the service of the Holland Company, as also all the European and Indian inhabitants, will be guaranteed the liberty of their persons and possessions, moveable and immoveable, merchandise and other effects will be held sacred and inviolable and will not be molested on any account.

Answer.—All private property shall be respected.

Article 5th.

In the preceding article is also included the Resident of Porca, Jan Andries Scheidzs, who happens to be in this town, and who has been employed to keep the books of trade concerning the liberty of persons and possessions, and after he has handed over the effects of the Company, he will be allowed to leave for Porcat, his residence, and there settle his affairs.

Answer.—He shall be allowed a reasonable time to settle his affairs, but must be considered as prisoner of war.

Article 6th.

The Commandant, the Members of Council, the Police, all the officers of Police, and of commerce, the Ecclesiastical Council, the Marine and other servants drawing pension will have the liberty to

* This, and succeeding articles, translated from the French.

depart with their families, slaves, and their properties and effects for Batavia, or for Colombo, and for the transport of these persons aforesaid, the necessary vessels and means for the voyage will be given at the expense of the English.

Answered in the second article.

Article 7th.

The capital or funds belonging to the Chamber of the Orphanage, to the poor of the Diaconie (? Deaconry) and to the Lepers' hospital will not be confiscated, but they will be maintained, as well as all the silver of the Minors or Pupils, and of the Poor.

Answer.—The funds mentioned shall be appropriated as His Britannic Majesty, or those empowered by him, shall direct.

Article 8th.

To all the officers, as well as to the Political and Civilian servants of the Company who are inclined to remain in this place, or to establish themselves in a certain place, to them will be accorded and they will enjoy the protection of the English flag.

Answer.—All the inhabitants, who choose to remain and take the oath of allegiance to His Britannic Majesty, shall be treated in every respect as British subjects.

Article 9th.

All the merchandise, munitions of war, artillery, and other arms, victuals in final all which belongs to the Company and that which is found in this place will be faithfully kept and delivered and will be received by the Commissioners, who alone are authorized to receive them, a specification of which in duplicate will be sent in due course to Mr. George Petrie.

Answer.—Everything specified in this article, shall be faithfully delivered to such persons, as Major Petrie may appoint, to be disposed of as His Britannic Majesty may direct.

Article 10th.

The fortress, the *commandement* (? Commandant's residence), the magazines, and other public buildings belonging to the Company will not be demolished, but retained in their present state.

Answer.—The fort of Cochin and all the public buildings must be disposed of as the Commander-in-Chief, or the Officer Commanding for the time being, shall direct.

Article 11th.

We will be allowed permission to exercise freely the reformed religion according to the custom of the Holland Church, for which use we will be allowed the church in which it has been practised up till now.

Answer.—Granted.

Article 12th.

The Veropoli convent, and all the other Roman Catholic churches, as well as the temples of the heathens will always enjoy the privileges which they have enjoyed until now under the protection of the Dutch Company (Compagnie Hollondoise).

Answer.—The British Government always protects every religious establishment.

Article 13th.

All the *Topas* (sepoys) and Christians, Indians, as also the Banyans, Orfeures (? Orfiores, Goldsmiths), painters, washermen (? or bleachers), cordonnieurs (? laceworkers or shoe-makers) who are subjects and vassals of the Ducth Company will have their properties protected and will always enjoy the privileges and protection which they have enjoyed as subjects of the company above stated.

Answered in the 4th and 8th articles.

* *Topasses*—Native Christian sepoys, dressed like European soldiers.

Article 14th.

All the chartered documents, resolutions and other papers belonging to and regarding the Commandant (or Government) of Cochin will be preserved and remitted without any one's inspection to Commander Vanspall, in short, he will be allowed to take them with him when he leaves.

Answer.—All public documents and papers must be delivered up to the persons appointed to receive them, but Mr. Vanspall shall receive authenticated copies of such as may in any shape relate to himself during his government of Cochin.

Article 15th.

No one will be lodged in the Commandant's residence during his stay in Cochin, but Mr. Vanspall, who will stay there without hindrance.

Answered in article 10th.

Article 16th.

If it should be found that there are any English deserters in the Cochin Garrison, they will be granted pardon.

Answer.—All deserters to be positively given up.

Article 17th.

All Public papers, Notarial and Secretariat Acts, which are liable to be destroyed in some way, for the surety of the property of the inhabitants of this place, they will be respected and preserved by those into whose hands they come, that present customs will be continued.

Answered in article 14th.

Article 18th.

The master of the public markets, the sequestrator, and the curator *adlities* will be maintained to settle debts and credits, and they will be under the protection of the ordinary Judges.

Answer.—All inhabitants, who shall remain in Cochin, shall be subject to the British laws.

Article 19th.

After the capitulation has been signed, the new port (Niew Poort) will be surrendered to an English guard of 50 men, with which will remain a Dutch guard of the same number of men, to remain during the arrangement of affairs, during which no Dutch soldier will be allowed to leave or an English one to enter, the day agreed on all the gates will be occupied and given over to the English while the garrison of Cochin retires to the barracks to remain until they depart for Batavia or Ceylon and will be deprived of their weapons, except the officers who will be allowed to retain them.

Answer.—The gates of the fort of Cochin shall be taken possession of by detachments of British troops, to-morrow at 12 o'clock noon. The garrison shall be lodged in as commodious a manner as circumstances will admit, till disposed of as mentioned in article the 2nd. The officers shall be allowed to retain their swords.

Article 20th.

All the servants of the Company, as well as those of the Police, and of the Militia, Marine and other servants drawing pensions will be maintained by the English Company, until they are carried in English vessels right to their destination, be it to Batavia or to Ceylon.

Answer.—Major Petrie does not conceive himself at liberty to come under any such engagement on account of the Honourable Company.

Article 21st.

All the sick and wounded found in the hospital will be maintained and cured by the English.

Answer.—Granted.

Major Petrie consents to a truce till 4 o'clock to-morrow morning, at which time Mr. Vanspall must declare his acceptance of or dissent to the above articles of capitulation." [182] In regard to the remarks in the preceding 3rd article, it must be stated, that slaves were not abolished in the British colonies till 1834.[183] Though the holding of slaves in British colonies was legal, it was nevertheless the case, as decided in 1772, that a foreign slave setting foot on British soil became free. An Act in Council in 1805 prohibited slave traffic in the conquered Dutch colonies. In 1824 it was declared piracy; and in 1837 it was punishable with transportation for life.

Along with Cochin, came the settlement at Tangacherry, and the various petty lands or pattams lying at distances up to 33 miles to the north and south. The pattams comprised Tumboli, Kattur, Attalakad, Manakodat, Antony (known as Kallancheri), Fernandez, Tekkepurupunkara, Mundenvelli, Domingo Fernandez Palakal, Santiago, Taiveppu, Belicho Rodrigues, Saint Louis, Duart Lemos, Hendrick Silva, Ramanturutti, Sondikalguvankure Silva, Palliport Hospital.[184]

In 1795 an English expedition left Madras, and landed at and captured Trincomalee. Jaffna and Calpentyn were also taken. A treaty was concluded with the king of Kandy, and a permanent footing in the island was gained.

It was stated that "From the manner in which the power of the Dutch has been exercised on the Island (Ceylon) and the impatience with which the king appears to have submitted to their controul, We are sanguine that His Majesty will be anxious to embrace an alliance, calculated, in a great degree, to relieve him from this inconvenience."

When the ambassadors were to appear before His Majesty the King of Kandy, the prime minister stated that he did not approve of "the plain and unadorned style in which he then beheld us, without further preamble, he then uncovered two trays or flat baskets on which were displayed two very rich and brilliant suits of brocade, made after a fashion in the European style, and two very large cocked Hats adorned with broad gold lace. It can easily be imagined, the figures we should have cut neither Hat or Cloathes, probably adopted to our size, but rather calculated to adorn some gross and corpulent Dutchman." They managed to avoid weaving them, by stating that "according to their superstitious notions, that a change of dress now, would be productive of some misfortune."

On being presented at court, they knelt along with the courtiers. After receiving permission to rise, the principal envoy, Mr. Andrews, was "about to relieve myself from the uneasy posture I had so long continued in, but was prevented from doing so, by its being notified that I must sollicit His Majesty's further permission, before I attempted to set down." After the request had been repeated, "not being permitted to sit with our legs across, we were made to adopt, as far as the pliability of our limbs would admit, the same position as the courtiers around us."

After conclusion of negociations, they returned to 'Trincomala' in their palankeen. When "it was set down for the relief of the bearers, the Inhabitants used to run up to it and although I was setting therein would immediately push their heads into it, and first look at me and then at the Palankeen with all the apparent astonishment expressed by a country clown at looking into a shew-box."

After the return of the ambassadors to Madras, they were followed by envoys from Ceylon, and the treaty was further considered.

---

[182] *Malbr. T.*, pp. 235–40. [183] *Mad. Manl. Admn.*, p. 504. [184] *Malbr. Manl.*, p. 715; *Malbr.*, Vol. ii., p. ccccxxii.

In the treaty made out by the King of Kandy, article 7 states :—" The Honorable English Company shall not either by fair or forcible means suffer the Dutch nation to have a possession of even so much as a Dust or an Inch of Land " in the Island of Ceylon. A hitch occurred in the negociations, chiefly on this point, on the Supreme Government remarking that, on the conclusion of the war, the Dutch settlements in Ceylon would probably have to be restored along with others, according to such terms as might be declared in the terms of peace ratified in Europe. The Ceylonese envoys were obstinate, and it was only by skilful diplomacy that the treaty was settled to the satisfaction of both parties.[185]

At that time, the Dutch position was that contained in a treaty which had been confirmed in 1766; but they considered themselves masters of the whole coast, and had never paid the tribute to the king, which the treaty provided for.[186]

Malacca was captured by the English during the same year.[187]

The year following the capitulation of Cochin, a separate Commissioner was appointed to administer the late possessions of the Dutch on the west coast of India. Under Dutch rule, the proprietary right in the soil was vested in Government; but the Dutch and Christian residents were exempted from ground-rent taxation. The land outside the Cochin fort was leased for twenty years, at the expiry of which it reverted to the Government. This system, slightly modified, was continued under British rule.[188]

A declaration, dated at Cochin, the 8th March 1796, and signed by "the Commissioner appointed for Cochin and the Dutch possessions on the Malabar Coast," defines the conditions under which they were to be administered :

"Whereas the Honourable the Governor in Council, with a view to give satisfaction and attending to the existing circumstances of their situation, is pleased to concede for the present to the Dutch European and Native inhabitants of Cochin and its dependencies the exercise and operations of their laws, customs and usages. It is hereby declared that a Fiscal, a Criminal and Civil Court shall be constituted with the usual formalities, and same power as heretofore practised under the late Dutch administration. Likewise, a Court of Appeals for the final decision of such civil cases as may be referred to it, the Commissioner to be President of the respective Courts, the members of which will be required to take the oath of allegiance to His Britannic Majesty so long as they shall remain under the protection of the British Flag. And it is further declared that, it is the determination of Government to maintain on their due footing the college for the guardianship of orphans and minors; the separate orphan house, the hospital for lepers at Paliport, the Matrimonial college, the pensions for widows who were in the receipt of them at the period of the capitulation, and that the Covenanted European and Native part of the Civil Servants, including the Medical and Ecclesiastical part of their establishment shall be entitled, for the time being, to the receipt of their pay as formerly allowed under their Company."

In the conditions for the lease of the export and import duties from and to the port of Cochin in 1796, article the twentieth states :—

" Under the late Netherlands' East India Company 4 per cent. was collected for the farmer and 1 per cent. for the Governor, and also upon some articles, a certain and fixed duty such as—

	RS.
1 chest opium	25
1 candy wild cinnamon	25
1 candy dry cocoanuts	1
1,000 fresh cocoanuts	1
1 chodena oil	1 silver fanam.

[185] *Mily. Sundry Book, No.* 89, 1795, 1796.
[186] *Mad. Manl. Admn.*, pp. 32, 118.
[187] *Mad. Manl. Admn.*, p. 31.
[188] *Malbr. Manl.*, pp. 511, 715.

	RS.
3,000 lbs. Cochin rice	8
75 parahs nelly	4
1 package of Colleche cloth	1
Timber	5 per cent.

which is now relinquished in favour of the farmer." [189]

Negombo and Colombo were stormed by the English. The last surrendered on articles by which the Dutch settlements were ceded to the English. The Ceylon settlements were thereafter administered from Madras.[190]

In the investigation which followed the treaty with Ceylon, the subject of slaves was discussed. It was stated "The number of slaves, the property of individuals, upon the Island of Ceylon, ought not to escape the notice of the British Government, altho' exclusively of those objections which must necessarily occur to their sudden Emancipation, as a measure of the State, it is absolutely precluded by the capitulation of Colombo, which expressly stipulates for the preservation of private property; but, as of all species of property, that of slaves would seem to present itself as the fittest object for taxation, and as it can only fall upon those who are well able to pay it, I would suggest that a tax be laid on slaves." Arrangements were to be made for its gradual abolition without attempting means which might be ruinous to the colonists.

Among other interesting particulars which the report contains, it is stated that "when the Portuguese established themselves on Ceylon commerce was not their only object. They wished to convert the natives of the Island to Christianity. Persons of the highest rank became the Sponsors when Cingalese Families were Christened and gave their names to the converts. This is the origin of the numerous Portuguese names which are found amongst the Cingalese. The Government of the Portuguese was oppressive, their reign turbulent, and after an almost uninterrupted series of bloody and disastrous wars it finished with conquest of their Territory by the Dutch with a very trifling force. The Dutch occupied themselves less with the conversion of the natives, although they employed a more successful method of making *nominal* Christians by giving certain offices to men of that Religion only. The Instruction given to these *official* converts was, however, too superficial to root out their prejudices in favour of the Idolatry of their ancestors." [191]

Descendants of the Portuguese and Dutch in Ceylon, yet retain their European customs, modified by long association with the natives among whom they live.

Palk's Strait, the north portion of the passage between the south of India and Ceylon, commemorates the name of a Dutch Governor.[192]

The British possessions in Guiana remained with the Dutch till 1796, when they surrendered to the English. Guiana was restored to the Dutch in 1802, but again taken by the English in the year following, since which, it has remained in their possession. [193]

Palkole and the other settlements in the Gódávari district, held by the Dutch under terms, were handed to the English in 1804.[194]

After the conclusion of the wars of the French Revolution (1789–1795), the majority of the Dutch East Indian colonies, which had been captured by the English, were restored to Holland, by the convention of the allied powers held in 1814. Cochin, Ceylon and the

[189] *Malbr. T.*, pp. 264, 265. [190] *Mad. Manl. Admn.*, pp. 32, 118.

[191] No. 25, R.D. Proceedings of a Committee of Investigation assembled at Colombo from 4th August 1797, p. 183.

[192] *Mad. Manl. Admn.*, pp. 2, 34. [193] *Mad. Manl. Admn.*, p. 504. [194] *Mad. Manl. Admn.*, p. 2; *God. Dt. Manl.*, p. 204.

Cape of Good Hope were excepted. The places included and handed over in 1818, were Sadras, Bimlipatam, Jaganadhapuram, Palkole, Porto Novo factory, Pulicat and Tuticorin. Malacca was also returned.[195]

The convention of the 13th August 1814, refers to the 1st January 1803, and states that the "Colonies, Factories, and Establishments which were possessed by Holland on that date, with certain exceptions, shall be restored, and the Right Honourable the Governor-General in Council has interpreted this reference to the 1st January 1803 to mean the possessions held by the Dutch East India Company in 1795."

"The chief rights and privileges were as follows :—

Bimlipatam.—Ground of the Fort and ruins of the factory with three bleaching grounds.

The Mint and Coinage of all coins—Gold, Silver and Copper.

Free trade and exemption from all duties and customs on exportation and importation. . . . .

Jugganatpooram.—Mint and right of coinage of Gold, Silver and Copper coins. . . . . .

Pulicat.—The ruins of the fort and factories, and ground on the beach on which the present flag-staff stands according to their ancient limits.

Mint and coinage of Gold, Silver and Copper coins.

Sadras.—Ruins of fort, town and port, with dependent villages and trade. . . . .

Tuticorin.—Various privileges including Mint and right of coinage in Gold, Silver and Copper." [196]

From 1819, till the final disappearance of competitive European powers from South India, the Madras Government was represented on the Coromandel Coast by a special agent, who was the medium of communication between that Government and the foreign settlements.[197]

By the treaty of March 1824, Malacca afterwards came back to the English, in exchange for the settlements at Bencoolen and other places on the west coast of Sumatra. By the treaty, it was also arranged that the Dutch should not interfere with the affairs of, or have any settlement in the Malay Peninsula. Java and the whole of Sumatra, excepting Achin, were ceded to them.[198]

Through this treaty also the whole of the Dutch South Indian settlements finally reverted to the English in 1825. Since that date, the Dutch have had no possessions in the Madras Presidency. The remaining towns thus rendered, were Sadras, Bimlipatam, Jaganadhapuram, Porto Novo factory, Pulicat and Tuticorin.[199]

---

[195] M.J.L.S., pp. 104, 125, 127 ; *Lists of Antiq.*, pp. 189, 308 ; *Chingpt. Dt. Manl.*, p. 90 ; *Tnvlly. Dt. Manl.*, p. 45 ; *Mad. Manl. Admn.*, p. 231.

[196] Report of Mr. John Hodgson appointed by the Right Honourable the Governor in Council of Fort St. George under date the 28th January 1818 to conduct the restitution of the Dutch Settlements situated in the Territories under the Presidency of Fort St. George.

[197] *Admn., Mad. Presidency*, p. 27.

[198] *Mad. Manl. Admn.*, pp. 2, 31.

[199] M.J.L.S., 1879, pp. 104, 125 ; *Lists of Antiq.*, pp. 189. 308 ; *Tnvlly. Dt. Manl.*, p. 45 ; *Chingpt. Dt. Manl.*, p. 90 ; *Mad Manl. Admn.*, pp. 1, 2 ; *Admn., Mad. Presidency*, p. 27.

PART II.—MONUMENTAL REMAINS.

CHAPTER IV.

DESCRIPTORY SKETCH.

MANY structural remains of the Dutch occupation of India, such as forts, private residences, warehouses and churches, yet exist in places. Those of the first class are generally either dismantled or ruined. Some of the others are still in use for the purposes for which they were built, but have been so altered or renovated, that their only interest is in the tradition connected with them.

The most interesting remains, are their tombs. The care and artistic skill bestowed on them, bear evidence to the reverence of the Dutch for their dead. This is further evidenced, as in the case of Sadras, where the treaty stipulated for the proper care of the tombs there. No less remarkable is the simple solidity of the construction of these quaint sepulchres, emblematic of the intention of the builders, that they would endure to the *laaste opstaanding*.

The tombs generally consist of great slabs of stone, either laid on the ground, or fixed on a substructure of brick and plaster. A few are placed under masonry mausoleums, such as in plates XXXVI, XXXIX (figures. 3, 4), and LXI : these, however, are exceptional. The majority of the stones are elaborately carved with coats-of-arms or monograms, and floral ornament with letters in *alto relievo*. In some cases, pieces of quaintly-sounding rhyme are added to the epitaph, such as are not uncommon among tombstones of the period in Scotland. At Masulipatam, even "the grave stone of an obscure *schipper* or sea captain, probably not of degree to bear coat armour, has an effigy of the deceased, with the three-cornered hat and long coat familiar in old illustrations."[200]

Wherever these tombs exist, they are executed in the same general style, and invariably evidence the work of the finished sculptor. Apart from their artistic merit, the work of cutting out the background, to the raised carving and lettering, must have been one of considerable labour. These tombs may have been partly cut by native workmen, but under the direction of trained European stone carvers. Much of the floral ornament is distinctly Indian in character: the coats-of-arms would require European supervision, if not actual execution. The stone is the species of hard hornblende on which Hindu inscriptions are generally cut. It has been suggested that the slabs were brought from Europe, but I know of no authority for the statement. Indeed, there seems no necessity why it should have been so, when the stone can be procured locally in abundance. The suggestion may, however, not so much apply to the slabs, as to the improbability of local labour being equal to the execution of the carving.

The patient labour bestowed on these monuments, and the imperishable nature of their construction, are in marked contrast to the unsubstantial commonplace brick erections of the English in India. "While the Portuguese and Dutch and Danish tombs still survive the power of the nationalities they represent" . . . . "English tombs have been too often flimsy in material and neglected utterly after construction."[201]

[200] *Kist. Dt. Manl.*, p. 100.

[201] M.J.L.S. 1878, p. 171.

Dr. Burnell writes on the subject:—"I was unable to seek out Leyden's tomb (at Batavia), but I doubt not that it is well cared for by the Dutch. In Java, at least, cemeteries are not allowed to be desecrated and become the abomination and disgrace they so often are in British India." [202]

Among the tombs of the seventeenth century in Masulipatam, there are none French or English, and "we must conclude either that the Dutch along this coast had more filial reverence for their deceased, or else that they, assuming a higher position, behaved more as if they were permanently established in the country." [203]

On a number of the drawings of the slabs herein illustrated, a portion only of the border ornament is shown. On the stones themselves, it is similarly repeated on all the four sides.

The chief historical events, relating to the places described in the succeeding chapters, have before been briefly detailed. They collectively followed the fortunes of the various European wars between England and Holland, and were successively taken, restored and re-taken by the former power. Thus, the later history of any one, is in effect, the same as that of the whole of them. These continued interruptions to the continuity of trade, must have had a serious effect on the commercial relations of the Dutch Company, and ultimately have been one of the chief factors which led to their decline. These repeated renditions latterly were looked on as so much a matter of course, that they came to be calculated on. In the negotiations of 1795-96, when the Ceylon envoys demanded the complete exclusion of the Dutch from the island, that they should not be allowed to possess "even so much as a Dust or an Inch of land in the Island of Ceylon," the Supreme Government demurred, on the probability of the Dutch Ceylonese possessions having to be again rendited on the conclusion of peace. The game only ended after the settlements had been rendered valueless, or unprofitable as places of trade to the Netherlands Company.

The records quoted in connection with the distress at Pulicat, are an example of what must oftimes have occurred at that and other places.

At several of the places, the monuments are fairly numerous; at other sites some few ruins exist; while as to others, only records or traditions attest there having been a settlement.

In contemporary records, quoting places by name, no attempt at transliteration is visible:— the varieties of spelling are as numerous as the records themselves, and vary with the periods when the latter were written.

CHAPTER V.

Bimlipatam.—A town on the Vizagapatam coast. The Dutch built a fort and factory in the middle of the seventeenth century. There are some tombstones dated 1623 in the old cemetery.[204] "The settlement of Bimlipatam is in fact little more than a factory, but it appears to have been a fortified factory. After being taken possession of in 1781 it was destroyed under orders received from England. No territorial jurisdiction is attached to this factory, but 3 washing greens belong to it and are the only appendages appertaining to this factory which appears to have

Note.—Mr. Alexander in a letter dated 8th January 1803 states the number of washing greens to be two, but the deed of restitution of 1785 mentions three.

[202] *S.I. Palae*, p. 49.   [203] *Kist. Dt. Manl.*, p. 104.   [204] *Mad. Manl. Admn.*, III, p. 96.

been merely a commercial factory or lodge with certain privileges. It is situated in the sea coast 14 or 15 miles North of Vizagapatam within the limits of the Zemindary of Vizianagrum and was granted to the Dutch Nation by the ancestors of the present Zemindar." [205] Some relics of its past importance remain, including the fort. [206]

CHAPTER VI.

CALICUT.—The capital of the Malabar district. Of the fort, no traces now remain. In 1846 there existed "a ruined doorway, the trace of a fosse and counter-scarp, some mounds marking the southern gateway, and the site of a few bastions." [207]

CHAPTER VII.

CANNANORE.—Fifty miles north-north-west of Calicut. In 1656 the Dutch effected a settlement, and built the present fort. [208] The fort is constructed of laterite, and is in good preservation. The Dutch factory, with its outwork on Mount D'eli, Dilly or Deli point, 16 miles to the north-west, commanded the river navigation of the north of the Kolattiri's dominions. [209] The Mount D'eli fort was first built by the Portuguese on a bluff projecting into the sea.[210]

CHAPTER VIII.

CHETWAI.—Fifty miles north of Cochin. A strip of land on the coast, insulated by the estuaries of Chetwai and Cranganore. The water communication at this place, at the mouth of a wide river, was contended for by the Portuguese and Dutch, and later by the English. In 1717 it was taken by the Dutch, who built a fort and made it the capital of their province of Pupinivattam.[211] Some few remains of the Dutch fort still exist. At the Chetwai bungalow, is the tombstone of Heer Wilhelm Blasser, sometime commandant of the fort there, who died in February 1729.[212]

CHAPTER IX.

COCHIN.—The old Dutch capital on the west coast. It was captured from the Portuguese by the Dutch in 1663. They greatly improved the place and its trade, building substantial houses, quays, &c. In 1778 Adrian Van Moens altered and improved the fort, with ditches and seven bastions.[213] There are the ruins of an old church converted into a cathedral in 1557. In 1806 the English blew up the cathedral, and destroyed some of the quays and the best houses in the fort. In the Protestant church are some curious old Portuguese and Dutch tombs. Ruins of the Portuguese fort still remain along the sea face.[214]

---

205 *Mad. Govt. Records, 'Hodgson's report'— Short Description of the Dutch Settlements*, para. 9.

206 *Mad. Manl. Admn.*, p. 253, M.J.L.S., 1879, p. 124, *L. Antiq.*, p. 14. 207 *Jour. As. Soc. Beng.*, XV, p. 224, *L. Antiq.* p. 246.

208 *Mad. Manl. Admn.*, III, p. 123 209 *L. Antiq.*, p. 241., Mallr., p. 8. 210 M.J.L.S., 1879, p. 120, *L. Antiq.*, p. 241.

211 *Mad. Manl. Admn.*, III, p. 166. 212 M.J.L.S., 1879, p. 116, Mallr., p. 9. 350, *L. Antiq.*, p. 250.

213 *Mad. Manl. Admn.*, III, p. 194. 214 *L. Antiq.*, p. 254, Mallr. II, CCCCXX.

CHAPTER X.

CONIMERE (Kunimedu).—On the South Arcot Coast, 13 miles north of Pondicherry. There is a Dutch tombstone close to the ruins of the old English factory, with the name Maria de Visser, and date 1703.[215] The following is a copy and interlined translation of the inscription :—

"HIER LEYT BEGRAVEN IUFER
Here lies buried Miss
MARIAD EVISSER HUYSVROW
Maria (de) Visser the wife of
VAN GERRIT WESTRENEN
Mr. Gerrit Westrenen
BOECKH OUDER INDIEN STDERE:
COMPE OVERLEDEN DEN CENIUNY
ANNO 1703 21 JAREN.
II MANDENEN JYDAGEN." [216]

CHAPTER XI.

CUDDALORE.—The head-quarters of the district of South Arcot. The fort once stood on the sea-shore, but is now half a mile inland, through recession of the sea. The place was latterly in possession of the English, but was formerly occupied by the Dutch. The factory of the latter, was situated 700 yards north of the fort. It seems to be first referred to, in the records for the the year 1678, and is again mentioned in those of years later. The English Fort St. David is referred to in early records as Tegnapatam, Thevanapatam, Devanapatam, Devanampatnam and Devipatnam. Garden house, the old residence of the Governor of the fort, was built in 1738; it still exists, and is used as a residence.[217]

CHAPTER XII.

DATCHEVARAM.—"This has ceased for a long time past to be a place of any note. It was a factory of which the ruins are still to be seen. Datchevaram is 8 or 10 miles west of Ingeram and Nillapilly." [218]

CHAPTER XIII.

JAGANADHAPURAM "is situated in the south bank of the Coconada river in the Bay of Coringa and between 90 and 100 miles south of Vizagapatam and 12 or 14 miles North of Ingeram, Yanam and Nillapilly. It is situated within the former limits of the Pettapore Zemindary.

Jugganautpooram is a small Town or rather a large Village with territory annexed thereto, and in 1781 appears to have been a place of some consequence. The factory house, fortified I believe, and all the publick buildings were demolished in that year, a considerable extent of salt pan ground is included within the limits of Jagganautpooram." [219] The place was originally known as Daatijeroon.[220]

---

[215] *S. Arcot Dt. Manl.*, p. 377. [216] List of European Tombs in the South Arcot District, 1893, p. 2.

[217] *Mad. Manl. Admn.*, p. 254, *L. Antiq.*, p. 211, M.J.L.S. 1879, p. 113.

[218] *Mad. Govt. Records,* *'Hodgson's report'—Short Description of the Dutch Settlements*, para. 11.

[219] *Mad. Govt. Records,* *'Hodgson's report'—Short Description of the Dutch Settlements*, para. 10. [220] *Gy. Dt. Manl.*, p. 196.

CHAPTER XIV.

MASULIPATAM.—Described in the records as Metchlepatam. The chief town of the Kistna district, standing near the coast, to the north of the delta of the Krishna river. The site of the early European settlements is situated among some salt marshes, about a mile nearer the sea, than the modern town now is. By tradition, the Dutch are said to have been the first to build the fort.

A description of the place in 1833 by Lieutenant Campbell states, that "the fort was originally built by the Dutch on a site (a patch of dry ground surrounded by a dismal swamp) which no living creature but a Dutchman, a frog, or an alligator, would ever have selected for his habitation." [221] The Dutch, however, had some villa residences, to which they were in the habit of retiring "out of Towne for better aire" than was afforded by their trading habitation in the swamp. This site is still known as Valandupalem, a vernacular derivative of Hollandpalem. [222]

There are a number of Dutch tombstones in various parts of the town. Some are plain slabs, but others are richly carved—in the style of those more particularly described at Pulicat—with raised and sunk lettering.

At Ramanapeta, three lie side by side in a small walled enclosure. The central one is a large slab, laid on a low pedestal, with an inscription and date 1701. The pedestals of the other two, are of similar shape, and built of brick and mortar.

In a large enclosure in the cantonment, are sixteen slabs. Some are sculptured and inscribed, and others quite plain. Their dates range from 1662 to 1743.

In the compound of the District Munsiff's court, is a carved slab, partly broken. It has an inscription and date 1640 (9 ?).

Copies and translations of the epitaphs of a few of these, have been made by Mr. Gordon Mackenzie, [223] and are here reproduced.

> "HIER LEYT BEGRAVEN DENE JACOB DEDEL, IN SYN LEVEN RAETVAN IN DIERST ENDE OPPER HOOFT TE WATER ENDE TE LANDE OVER DE NEDERLANTZE E. COMP. DESER CUST CORMANDEL. OVERLEDEN, DEN 29 AUGUSTY ANNO 1624.
>
> (Here lies buried the Hon. Jacob Dedel, in his life Councillor in the service and chief by water and by land of the Dutch India Company on the Coromandel Coast. Died August 29th. 1624.)"
>
> "DESE ZERK BEGRYPT ONDER ZIG DE DOODE LICHAMEN VAN CATHARINA VAN DEN BRIEL VAN AMSTERDAM EN JOHANNES KRUYF VAN TOUANAN ONDERKOOPMAN IN DIENST DER E. COMP. JONGE DOGTER EN IONG MAN GEBOREN DEN 15 AUG. 1657 EN 28 NOV. 1649 OVERLEDEN HIER TEN CONTOIRE 3 OCTOBER 1678 EN I JANUARY 1679 OUT 21 JAREN IMAEN 19 DAAGENEN 29 IAREN IMAEN 3 DAAGEN.

[221] *Kist. Dt. Manl.*, pp. 99, 114. [222] *Kist. Dt. Manl.*, p. 100. [223] *Kist. Dt. Manl.*, pp. 99–104.

REQUIESCANT IN PACE.

EEN VRYER EN EEN MAEGD BEDECKT
DEES EENE STEEN
HAER BEYDER MENING WAS VAN TWEETF
WORDEN EEN.
MAER DE OVERWREDE DOOD BELETTE VERGAREN
EERST GAF DEN BRIEL HET OP, EN DOE WIERD KRUYF
EEN LYK.
HAER LYVEN ROTTEN HIER MAER INDES HEMELS RYCK.
ZAL GOD DE ZIELEN VAN DE TWEE GELEVEN PAREN.

(Buried under this slab are the dead corpses of Catharine Van Den Briel of Amsterdam and John Kruyf of Tounan, junior merchant in the service of the Hon. Comp., a young woman and young man, born the 15th August 1657, and 28th November 1649, died at the factory here the 3rd October 1678, and 1st January 1679 aged 21 years, 1 month and 19 days, and 29 years, 1 month and 3 days.

May they rest in peace.

A lover and a maid this one stone covers; their mutual meaning was of two to make one; but too cruel death forbad the union First Den Briel gave it up and then Kruyf became a corpse; their lives lie here, but, in Heaven's Kingdom, shall God the Souls of these two persons pair.)

HET DODE LICHAAM VAN JUFFRW JONNA BOLWERK IN HAAR LEVEN HUISVROW VAN DEN KOOPMAN ENTWEDE HIER TEN CONTOIRE SR JOHANNES HUYSMAN RUST ONDER DESE ZERK OVERLEDEN DEN 16 EN FEBRUARY A. 1682 OUD. 43 IAREN 11 MAANDEN EN 8 DAGEN.

TER WYL IK LEEFDE HIER BENEDEN,
HAD IK D'ELLINDE TOT MYN LOT
MET ZIEKTEN WIERD IK STEEDS BESTREDEN
TOT DAT HET DEN ALWYZEN GODT
GELIEFDE MYNE ZIEL IN VREDEN
TE PLAATZEN BY DER ENGLEN ROT
DAAR LEV' IK VRY VAN ZIEKT, EN PUYNE
GEEN BETER RUYLING ALS DE MYNE.

This dead corpse of Miss Jane Bolwerk, in her life, wife of the merchant, second in charge of the Factory here, Mr. John Huysman, rests under this slab.

While I lived here beneath,
Had I to suffer my lot,
With sorrow was I ever bested,
Until the all wise God
Was pleased my soul in peace
To place by the angel choir,
There I am free from pain,
No better exchange than mine.

HET DODE LICHAAM YAN IUFFER ELIZABETH VAN ERPECUM IN HAAR LEVEN WAARDE HUISVROW VAN SR MÁRTEN VAN DEN BRIEL ONDER KOOPMAN EN ADMINISTRATEVOR DER SPECERY PAKHUIS EN ALHEIR WAGT ONDER DESE SERK D'URE DER LAASTE OPSTAANDING. SYSTORF DEN 17 EN FEBY. 1685 EN WAS OUT 60 JAREN. BELESEN, DEUGDSAAM, VROOM, STANDVASTIG VAN GEMOET.

NIETLIGT VERANDER LYK DOOR VOOR OF TEGEN WINDEN DEN AMSTEL WAS HAAR WIEG, DAAR WIERD SY OPGEVOET,

HIER STORF S'IN GOD VERNOEGD, VAN DAGEN SAT EN IAREN,

HAAR VROME ZIEL SAL MET DE CHERUBYNEN PAREN.

The dead corpse of Miss Elizabeth Van Erpecum, in her life worthy spouse of Mr. Marten Van Den Briel, junior merchant and warehouse-keeper, here waits under this slab the hour of the resurrection. Died the 17th February 1685, and was aged 60 years. Cultured, virtuous, pious, steadfast of mind, not lightly changeable by winds to and fro, the Amstel was her cradle, there she was brought up, here dead, she in God happily, full of days and years, her pious soul shall with the cherubim pair.

DIES STEIN BEDECKT DE ROMPEN VAN DEN E. HR. JACOB CORBESIER GEBOORTIG VAN VYTRECHT IN SYN LEVEN COPPERCOOPMAN IN DIENST DERE. COMP. EN GEELIEFERT SECUNDE BY DEN ED. HEER GOUVERNEUR TOT PALLIACATTA OBIIT ALHIER DEN 15 AUGUSTUS 1687 OUD SYNDE OMTRENT 51 IAREN.

IUFFR MARGARIETA BOOMS VAN AMSTERDAM SYNE SALIGERS HUYSVROUWE. ALHIER GESTURVEN DEN 24 EN AUGUST 1687 OUD OMTRENT 46 IAAREN. SR. ADRIEN BLOCKEEL VAN YSSENDYCK SYNDE GEWEEST ONDER COOPMAN IN GEMELTEN DIENST EN OPPER HOOFD VANT, COMPTOIRE DAETCHEROM ALDAER OVERLEDEN DEN 19 MAY 1687 OUD SYNDE OMTRENT 40 IAAREN.

IVER ELIZABETH FRONTENIUS GEBOORTIG TOT PALLIACATTA SYN HUYSVRO O WE EN DOCHTER VAN VOORNOEMDE IUFFR ALHIER ONTSLAPEN DEN 24 MAERT 1688 OUD OMTRENT 21 IAAREN.

SR WILHELM FRONTENIUS MEDE VAN PALLIACATTA IN SYN LEVEN ASSISTANT IN DIENST DER E. COMP. EN BROEDER VAN DE IUFR VERDRONCKEN TUSSCHEN DEES PLAETZE EN PALLICOL DEN 14 OCTOBER 1687 OUD SYNDE RUYM 31 IAAREN.

IACOBUS CORBESIER DELONGE GEBOORTING, TOT DAETCHEROM SOON VAN EERST GENOEMDEM HR EN

IUFR MEDE ALHEIR OVERLEDEN DEN 21 SEPTEMBR 1687 OUD SYNDE OMTRENT 7 IAAREN.

SOO DAT HIER LEGGEN EEN VADR EEN MOEDER.
EEN SUSTER TWEE BROEDERS
TWEE MANNEN EN TWEE WYVEN
DOCH NIET MEER DAN SES LYVEN.

This stone covers the corpses of the Hon. Mr. James Corbesier, native of Utrecht, in his life senior merchant in the service of the Hon. Company, and elevated as second by the Hon. the Governor of Pulicat, died here the 15th August 1687, aged about 51 years; Mrs. Margaret Booms of Amsterdam, his late wife, died here the 24th August 1687, aged about 46 years: Mr. Adrien Blockeel of Issendyck, formerly junior merchant in the above-mentioned service, and chief of the factory at Daetcherom, died there the 19th May 1687, aged about 40 years.

Mrs. Elizabeth Frontenius, native of Pulicat, his wife and daughter of the above-mentioned dame, fell asleep here the 24th March 1688, aged about 21 years.

Mr. William Frontenius, also of Pulicat, in his life assistant in the service of the Hon. Company, and brother of the lady, drowned between this place and Palicol, the 14th October 1687, aged more than 31 years.

Iames Corbesier Delonge, native of Daetcherom, son of the first-named husband and wife also died here the 21st September 1687, aged about 7 years

So that here lie, one father, one mother,
One sister, two brothers,
Two men and two wives,
But not more than six lives.

ZY SULLEN RUSTEN OP HERE SLAAP-STEEDEN.
IES–57–2.

HIER RUST EEN VROWE, DOOR DE DOOD
GESCHEYDEN VAN HAAR EGT—GENOOT
IN BITTREN ROOW, BESTELD TER AARDE
BE WEEND MET TRANEN VLOED. NA WARDE.

ONDER DESEN ZARK LEGT BEGRAVEN M'IUFF MARIA WILHELMINA GAMBIER ZALR GEMALINNE VAN DEN EE HEER GOSEWYN MAIRE OPPERCOOPM. SECUNDE TE DESER CUSTE CHOROMANDEL EN OPPERHOOFD DIT NOORDER DISTRICT NATA TER STEEDE NAGAPATNAM DER 15TH OCT. 1702, OBIIT ALHIER TOT MASULIPATNAM DEN 2 AUGUSTY AO 1735 OUD 32 IAREN 9 MAANDEN EN 18 DAGEN.

They shall rest in their beds—Isaiah 57, 2.
Here lies a wife, through death
Separated from her husband

In bitter ruth, bestowed to earth
Bewailed with flood of tears, according to worth.

Under this slab lies buried Mrs. Maria Wilhelmina Gambier, late wife of the Hon. Mr. Gose Wyn, Mayor, senior merchant, second of this Coromandel Coast and first of this Northern District. Born at Negapatam, October 15th 1702, died here at Masulipatam, the 2nd August 1735, aged 32 years, 9 months and 18 days.

CHAPTER XV.

NARSAPUR.—The head-quarters of the taluk of that name in the Gódávari district. There are the remains of an old fort. The Dutch had an iron foundry in 1665. The ground on which the Dutch factory stood, was washed away by the river Gódavari some years ago. [224]

CHAPTER XVI.

NEGAPATAM.—A seaport, still of some importance, and a terminus of the South India Railway, 48 miles east of Tanjore. It was taken from the Portuguese by the Dutch in 1660, and became their chief seat on the Coromandel coast. The ruins of their old fort are surrounded by a ditch partly filled up. [225] In the walls of the Kailasanatha temple is inserted a stone with a Dutch epitaph dated 1777.[226]

The cemetery is a long rectangular enclosure containing a number of Dutch and a few English tombs (pl. I.). Some of the former, with dates extending from 1664 to 1788, are illustrated on plates II to XIII. Plates III, IV, VII and IX are from drawings, the others are fac-simile impressions. In the drawings, a portion only of the border ornament is shown. On the stones, the carving is repeated on all the four sides.

CHAPTER XVII.

PALAKOL, PALKOLE OR POLICOLE.—"Is situated on the south bank of the Narsapore river, a branch of the Godavery, about 7 miles from Narsapore and between 40 or 50 miles south of Jagganautpooram but not far from the English factory of Maddepollam. The factory house and buildings were destroyed when the factory was taken possession of in 1781. There is a small extent of territorial jurisdiction attached to Policole and a piece of ground depending thereon at Narasapore. The Town of Policole contains about 1,000 houses and about 300 Looms."

"The settlements of Bimlipatam, Jagganautpooram and Policole are represented to be held under Fermans granted by the Nizam and confirmed by the Mogul or Emperor of Delhi, bearing various dates from A.D. 1628 to A.D. 1713 and by a Cowle granted by Hajee Houssun in A.D. 1734 and A.D. 1752 by Jaffur Ally Khan. The two last mentioned persons were Naibs or deputies of the Nizam in the Circars. The Dutch are stated to have first occupied these factories about the year A.D. 1628." [227]

---

[224] *L. Antiq.*, p. 41. M.J.L.S., 1879, p. 125. *Mad. Manl. Admn.*, *III*, p. 565.

[225] *Mad. Manl. Admn.*, III, p. 581.

[226] *L. Antiq.*, p. 281 ; Pl. XII.

[227] *Mad. Govt. Records*, '*Hodgson's report'—Short Description of the Dutch Settlements*, paras. 12, 13.

The soil around is fertile, and the Dutch largely cultivated oranges, pumplemosses, and plantains. In the quiet little cemetery, shaded by orange trees, are several Dutch tombstones in good preservation. Copies and translations of two of the oldest are given.[228]

"HIER LIYE BE GRAVEN DZOON VAN DEN ADST. LAMBERT HEMSINCK GENGERRALRI, GEBOREN IN PALICOL ADIJ 17 DEN OCTOBER Ao 1660 EN OVERLEDEN DEN 9 DEN NOVEMBER Ao 1662.	Here lies interred the son of the Assistant Lambert Hemsinck Gengerralri, born in Palicol 17th October Ao 1660 deceased 9th November Ao 1662.
HIER LEYT BEGRAVEN SYMON VAN GROENEWEGEN VAN DELFT IN SYN LEVEN COOPMAN EN OPPERHOOFT TEN COMPTORE PALICOL OBIJT ADIJ 3 EN IONIJ Ao 1665.	Here lies interred Symon Van Groenewegen of Delft, during his life merchant and chief of the factory, Palicol, died 3rd June Ao 1665."

CHAPTER XVIII.

PAMBAN.—On the seashore at Pamban, at the west of the island of that name, is a fort, with parts of the walls in fair preservation.[229] It is said to have been constructed by the Dutch about 1653.

In a letter from the Commercial Resident at Ramnad, to the Board of Trade at Fort St. George, dated 17th April 1817, mention is made of the Dutch possession of the fort. "In Pambon, as your Board will observe by the enclosed copy of a letter from my Moneagar of that Part, there is an old Fort, which, it is said, was once taken by the Dutch and afterwards re-taken by the former Sadoopady or Rajah of Ramnad, but it is represented to be now in a very ruinous state."

CHAPTER XIX.

PORTO NOVO.—"Is a factory or Commercial lodge situated on the North Bank of the Porto Novo or Coleroon River. It appears to have suffered frequently during the Wars of the Carnatic and altho' restored in 1785 seems never to have been re-established as a place of trade. The factory house is still standing, but was claimed as private property in the year 1806 by a Mr. Topander, a Dutch Gentleman. The Sannads or deeds under which the factory of Porto Novo was established and its establishment confirmed are numerous :—

From Mr. Hyde, dated 7th March 1818.

A.D. 1643.	A Cowle granted by the Commander of the forces at Gingee.	
" 1644.	do.	the Naick of Gingee.
" 1651.	do.	the King of Viziapoor or Bijeanuggur.
" 1654.	do.	the Commander of the Bijeanuggur forces at Gingee.
" 1664.	do.	do. do.

228 *Gódy. Dt. Manl.*, p. 197.

229 *Mad. Manl. Admn.* III, p. 666.

A.D. 1677.	A Cowle granted by	Sevajee, Conqueror of Gingee.
,, 1680.	do.	the Commander of the Troops of Raganaut Row.
,, 1694.	do.	Sulfear Khan.
,, 1745.	do.	Anwardeen Khan, Nabob of the Carnatic."

"All the settlements of the Dutch East India Company enumerated above appear to have been very ancient possessions of the Dutch Nation—dates relating to them have been traced on the English East India Company's Records to A. D. 1624, 1647, 1680, 1688, 1690 down to the deeds of restoration for all of them executed in 1785."

"The Dutch Company and their factors carried on at one time an extensive trade in Cloths and other articles, and the Country generally must have greatly benefitted by the mutual exchanges of goods and merchandize to which their trade led."[230] The Dutch had a bleaching place called **Wannarpalaiyam.** There are some Dutch tombs here, of which the following are copies. :—

There are also eleven others uninscribed.[231]

"CHRISTUS IS MIJU, LEVEN, STERVEN IS MIGN GEROIN, VROUW MARGARITHA HACKAART, ZEERWAAR DEGEMALUME VANDEN E. MATTHYS PFÚFFER IS GEBOREN TOT PALLIACATTA, PRIMO JANUARY, ANNO 1698 EN OVERLEDENDEN 19 DECEMBER ANNO 1730.

HAAR URSTE SOONTJE GENAMPT IASPER THEODORUS PFÚFFER GEBOREN TOT—I PORTO—NOVO DEN 17, DECR. ANNO 1777 EN OVERBDEN DEN 24 DITO SUSANA PFÚFFER GEBOREN MEDEALDAAR ANNO 1726, DEN 15TH FEBRY. EN GESTORVEN ULTIMO MAART A.O. 1727.

ANNO 1724 DEN 4TH APRIL IS GEBOREN TOT NAGAPATNAM, CATHARINA WILLEMINAIANDER BURG BEHOUD DOCHTER TGI VANDEN HAVEN GENI EN OVERBDEN DEN 20 DECR. A.O. 1731. DUS STERN BE DEKT HET RIF MAN MOLDER DOCHTERS ZOON HAAR ZIELEN ZIGN OM LIVOG BIJ GOD INS HEBUELS FROON WIL ZALIG IS DE MENSH WENS LEVEN HEIR ZOO EENDI MET UOORSMAAK VAN GOD'S VRENGD BEVRIJD VANAL ELENDI."

"LET OP DEN VROOMEN EENDI, SIET NADEN OP REGTEN, WANT HET EYNDEAN DIEN MAN SAL VRUDE ZYN! P.S. 37. 37. DO VREEDE LEEV END' WAS STUDS IN WILMINENDHEYD EN IDER' TZYNE GAF ENDOOR GEDUNS TIGHEYD ELLKS HARTE TOTSIG TROG RUST NUTE DESER HAVEN, DOG ZYN GEDAG TENISS BLYFD BY OUS ON BIGRAVEN HONDER DESEN ZARKE RUST, SR. WILLEN SPITS, IN DISSELF. SEVEN BOCK, CASENFACTUUR, HONDER, TEN DESEN, COMPTOIRE PORTO—NOVO, GEBOOREN TOT NAGAPATNAM DEN 13TH DECEMBER ANNO 1684 EN ALHR OVER LEDEN DEN 20 JULY ANNO 1737 OUD 52 JAREN 7 MAANDENEN 7 DAGEN."[232]

---

[230] Mad. Govt. Records. *Hodgson's Report—Short Description of the Dutch Settlements*, paras. 16 to 18.

[231] M.J.L.S., 1879, p. 125, *S. Arcot. Dt. Manl.*, p. 377. *Mad. Manl. Admn.* III, p. 712.

[232] *List of European tombs in the South Arcot District*, 1893, p. 2.

CHAPTER XX.

PULICAT.—"Is situated 25 miles North of Madras on the south bank of the lake of Pulicat, and River running from the lake to the sea. It was after the cession of Negapatam to the English the Chief Settlement of the Dutch East India Company on the coast of Coromandel and when I visited it in 1796 possessed a small but strong Fort with many useful buildings within the walls. The fort and buildings were destroyed in 1805 or 1806 soon after the news was received in India of the annexation of Holland to the French Empire. An Island in the lake with a fine Village thereon, and three other Villages are dependent on Pulicat. The Dutch authorities of Pulicat have therefore territorial jurisdiction over Pulicat proper and its limits, and over four other Villages and their limits. One street of the Town only belonged to the Dutch Nation. The other part of the Town formed a part of the territory of the Carnatic. Pulicat is stated to have been first occupied by the Dutch in A. D. 1612 and possession thereof to have been obtained under an agreement made with the then Rulers of the Carnatic. Various privileges are stated to have been granted by the same authority in A. D. 1643 and 1646, to have been confirmed by Firmauns from the Nizam, dated A. D. 1686; and in A. D. 1689, 1712 and 1713 to have been further confirmed by a deed executed in behalf of the Mogul, or Emperor of Delhi.[233] References have been made (*ante*) to its mercantile importance both before and during the Dutch occupation. Traditions still exist as to the opulence of the former inhabitants. A street with large and pretentious houses still stands as a memorial of the extensive trade once carried on. Of these mansions, some are entirely deserted; in others solitary individuals have made their abode; while a few are divided and occupied by a number of families. On account of the distress caused to the Dutch inhabitants at Pulicat by the long continuance of the war, a committee was appointed in 1813 to investigate the matter on the spot. In the report, it was stated (Ar. 2) that "the place is greatly reduced in wealth, in manufactures and population and that the immediate objects of our enquiry the Servants of the Dutch East India Company are, without exception, reduced to poverty and in many instances loaded with debt."

They had been living in "the delusive hope of seeing the Dutch flag re-established."

In carrying out measures of relief, it was proposed that they be divided into "two great classes of white, and men of color"; the former were to get an allowance of 30 pagodas, and the latter 15 pagodas.

"There is no doubt that the sum of pagodas 5 per month fixed for the assistants or writers, is very small for the support of a half-cast family, their taste for dress is proverbial, and in many instances they are very numerous, but our enquiries here have led us very much to doubt, whether a small increase of salary would not tend more to the increase of dissipation than to any real benefit of the family to which it was granted."

Some of those who got their living by fishing, had been prevented doing so, and on a suit being decided against them their houses were pulled down, "the materials were sold, even their cloths, Brass pots, Boats, Nets, Fowls and the Eggs, on which they were sitting, in short, that everything was disposed of and the miserable inhabitants compelled to seek a livelihood in other countries."

A number of persons were recommended for allowances. Among them was Mr. Mey Kamp, who was in receipt of an "allowance of Pagodas 14-2-60. He is officiating Reader in the Calvinist Church and his family consists of his wife and Eight domestics; we

---

[233] Mad. Govt. Records. *Hodgson's Report—Short Description of the Dutch Settlements*, para. 14.

recommend that his allowance be fixed at the rate of 20 Pagodas per month to enable him while in the situation to associate with the first class of the Inhabitants."

Accompanying the papers is a petition from the Dutch inhabitants translated by I. McDonall, Dutch Translator. It seems, from various references, that a Dutch Translator was employed by the Madras Government. This would be necessary, for, though some of the correspondence between the Governments is in French, a large proportion of that received is written in Dutch.

The flourishing trade of the town seems, after the final occupation of the English, to have gradually deserted it, and migrated with its merchants to Madras. During its period of prosperity, it stood on the seashore, but now, through drifting sand, it is a mile inland.[234] The recession of the sea was fatal to its existence as a seaport, and the proximity of the superior facilities of Madras naturally caused its trade to be diverted in that direction.

In a report, previously quoted (paragraph 55), by Mr. Hodgson appointed by the Government of Madras in 1818 to conduct the restitution of the Dutch settlements, it is mentioned that "the town of Pulicat is divided into two parts—one part being a street composed of buildings after the European fashion and chiefly occupied by the Dutch inhabitants is within the Dutch limits, the other part is within the limits of the Carnatic territory and was not any time ceded to the Dutch."

Of the works of the early Dutch settlers, some few yet remain.

The fort, or "Castle Geldria," which has been a square brick structure with bastions on the angles and faces, and enclosed by a wide and deep moat, has very little but the site remaining. The moat still exists unimpaired. The fortifications themselves have been completely razed, and only some few masses of dismantled and fallen brickwork project in places through the soil. From its small area, there can have been no considerable settlement inside the fort itself. The settlers, if numerous, may have resided outside the walls. It was probably, simply a place of refuge, or citadel to enclose and protect the factory. A pictorial representation appears on plate XXIX.

In an enclosure, outside and west of the fort, is the Dutch cemetery, (plate XIV) containing many quaintly carved tombs (pls. XV and XVII to XXXIX), walled-in and kept in perfect order and preservation by Government. The enclosed space slightly exceeds half a Dutch acre of ground. A quaint and interesting Romanesque lichgate forms the entrance at the south-east corner (plate XVI). On each side of this gateway, a square pilaster, abutting on the court walls, supports a semi-circular arch. Over, is a horizontal classical cornice with a ball finial on each outer ledge. It is surmounted by a curved moulded tympanum, open in the centre to receive a carved and foliated vase. The pilasters have a moulded base; and capital, with egg-and-dart ornament between two Ionic volutes or scrolls. On the front of each of the two pilasters, is a standing skeleton, almost life-size. One has an hour-glass on his head, and the other supports a skull on a column. Carved on the key-stone or central voussoir at the arch crown, is a winged death's-head with hour-glass. On the left front face of the archivolt, is a Latin quotation from the Apocalypse, in Roman letters of the 17th century: the translation is elsewhere given. On the corresponding right curve of the arch, is an inscription in Dutch, with the date 1656.[235]

The old church is a building of no special architectural note. On its south side, is an old sun-dial. (Plate XXXIX, fig. 5.) The pedestal is of plastered masonry, with a

[234] *Mad. Manl. Admn.*, p. 254.

[235] G.O., No. 219, P., 4th March 1889.

granite slab on the top, into which the dial is fixed. The dial itself is a teak board with iron supports.

The accompanying plates do not represent the whole of the tombs, but only illustrate a selection from the most characteristic and interesting. Most of the stones in the cemetery are both carved and inscribed in raised letters. Some are inscribed, but are devoid of carving. There are a few English stones placed along the west boundary, with dates ranging from 1829—just subsequent to the English occupancy of Pulicat—to 1872.

Most of the slabs lie on the ground without any covering; others are surmounted by a brick and plaster structure. Of the latter, two are shown on plate XXXIX. Figure 3 surmounts the stone shown on plate XXXVII, and figure 4 that on plate XXXI. They are low open structures resting on piers. They are moulded in stucco. Others of a solid and more lofty structure, are the cenotaphs on figures 1 and 2 of the same plate. The mausoleum on plate XXXVI stands over the slab XXXII. It is erected to one of the Governors, and is the most imposing of any at the place. It has an open vaulted roof, and rests on twelve-arched piers. The superstructure is ornamented in stucco, with flying cherubs, flower vases at the corner pilasters, and surmounting vases. Plates XVII, XX and XXXVIII are *fac-simile* estampages. The following English translations are by Dr. Jas. Burgess :—

PLATE XV.

(Round the Monogram N.P.)

" When me to life * brought I numbered ten and eight years."
Here lies buried Neeltje Pieterson
Daughter of Captain Pieter Huberechtson
And the wife of Cornelius Van Wede
Died the first October, Anno 1655.

PLATE XVI.

(On the lich gate,)

" Blessed are they who die in the lord
They rest from their labour. "

Apocalypse, Chapter XIV, v.-13.

PLATE XVIII

Here lies buried Peter Matheusson Captain of the East India Company, of the Yacht Saphir, aged 51 years. Died 9th February 1658.

PLATE XIX.

Underneath lies buried Abraham Carter
of Rotterdam, in his lifetime merchant
in the service of the United Dutch East
India Company, aged 40 years. Died the
13th June Anno 1660.

* Eternal life.

PLATE XXI.

Hereunder lies buried Pieter Monsieur Huybertsen of Rotterdam, in his lifetime Captain in the service of the United East India Company. Died the 21st March, Anno 1669, being about 70 years old.

Also here lies buried Lady Assensa Pieteren wife of the above-named Captain Pieter Huybertsen. Died the 2nd September Anno 1669, being 68 years old or thereabouts.

PLATE XXII.

Here lies buried the Lady Ceertruydt Duraeus, in her lifetime wife of the under-merchant Jacob Van Al Monde,—Died the 30th October 1671, 28 years and 9 months old.

PLATE XXIII.

(Latin).

(Place of) Sepulture.

Of the most pure and pious Lady Jacomina Baffart the greatly beloved wife of M. Marten.Pit, who died of childbirth A.C. Mdclxxiii, the 18 October, leaving an only little daughter Jacomina Pit, who survived her mother by two days.

PLATE XXIV.

Here lies buried the Lady Catharina Blockhovius, wife of the merchant Sieur Jacob Corbisier; died the 10th November Anno 1675, being 29 years and 20 days old.

PLATE XXV.

(In 4th line the reading may be "Saliger Her Gules," or "Saliger Hercules"? (I am doubtful which is correct.)

This burial place contains the body (skeleton) of the pure Lady Sara Linden born . . . daughter of the deceased Mr. Jules (Hercules(?)) Linderborn in his life Captain of the "Borgerij" (town guard) at Colombo, closing her life on the last of December Anno 1673, aged 17 years 2 months and 12 days.

Virgin.

Sara was only dust and ashe S
All in a short time (? hardly translatable) A
Death calls us with her togethe R
Amen, God's grace lives in SarA.

(These 4 lines form a doggerel acrostic on the name Sara, having the letters at the beginning, middle, and end of it).

Also lies hereunder the Honourable young daughter Elizabeth, Lindeborn, born the 25th November 1660; and at Palliacota, the 27th May 1677, died, being only so old (as) 16 years, 6 months, minus one day.

PLATE XXVI.

Hereunder lies buried Joannes Verkerck, a native of Delf, in his lifetime under-merchant and second person in the Kingdom of Pegu, here at Palliakatta died the 12th March, Anno 1678, being about 46 years old.

PLATE XXVII.

Burial place.

Of the most noble Mr. Jacques Cuillier, in his lifetime Governor and Director of the Coast of Kormandel and the circuit of the same, born in the town of Ghent, 1620, died at ("tot") Paleakatta, Anno 1679, the 5th November, 59 years 8 months and 12 days old.

The Governor Jacques rests.

With two of his name and twice two, born of two different mothers.

This sacred resting place gives an enduring fame.
Joanna closes this blessed list
also sisters and brothers.

(Some Latin words illegible). J.B.

PLATE XXVIII.

Here lies buried the Honourable Lady Joanna Berio, widow of the deceased Honourable Abraham Floriszoon Bolwerk, in his lifetime "visitor of the sick" (perhaps an official title) at Masulipatam; born in Amiens, 17th September 1614, and died the 18th May 1684, being 70 years old.

PLATE XXIX.

Here lies buried Abraham Mendis, in his lifetime merchant, born in the State (? City) Oetacotta, obiit the 5th April 1684, 48 years old.

PLATE XXX.

The noble Heer Willem Van Dielen overmerchant, second over Coromandel, and chief of Masulipatam, &c. Born at Haarlem the 5th August, Anno 1650, and died at Palliacatta, the 13th October Anno 1688; also his little daughter Catharina Van Dielen 5 years old, and a little son 24 days old; both died shortly before their father.

PLATE XXXI.

Hereunder lies buried Jan Martenszoon, in his lifetime merchant in the service of the E. Company and chief of the Comptoirs Palliacatta, born the 21 June 1667, and died the last of March A. 1717, aged 49 years 9 months and 10 days.

Here rests he who had no resting
so long as he was in life,
with all the temporal weary and tired,
his soul to God again has he given,
in order with him in eternity
to obtain joy among the inhabitants of Heaven,
to taste the blessedness prepared
for those who die in the Lord.

PLATE XXXII.

"Ye shall rest and stand in your lot," Dan. 19, v. 13: here lies buried Dirk Both, deceased in his lifetime merchant and chief in this Castle of Geldria at Palliacatta, born at Utrecht 29th March 1666, and here died the 24th June A. 1719, aged 31 years 2 months and 26 days.

The cold bones of both lie under this slab,
he departs from turmoil and all the vain work,
in order at God's right hand to obtain rest,
O blessed lot of those that die in the Lord.

PLATE XXXIII.

Under this slab lies buried the Lady Sara Jorin, spouse of Cornelis De Munt, merchant and chief of this Castle of Geldria at Palliacatta. Born the 17th April Anno 1681, and died the 20th July Anno 1723, aged 42 years 3 months and 3 days.

"Weep with those that weep." (Rom. 12, 15.)
Here Munts laid down pleasure, enjoyments, delights,
and all that was dear to him in the world's tearful vale.
He was afflicted in bitter sorrow: help to weep his loss.
God strengthen his soul and give him consolation.

PLATE XXXIV.

"We fall off as a leaf." Isaiah, 64, v. 6 Mr. Gallart's worthy spouse, escaped from all pain and sorrow, separated from him by death, rests under this stone in peace. Willing and well-prepared, transplanted ("flitted") out of all earth's turmoil, she now enjoys blessedness, her everlasting inheritance in the heavens.

Here lies buried:

Lady Anna Margaretha Moller, deceased spouse of Mr. Michiel Gallart, merchant and chief at this Castle of Geldria at Palliacatta, born at the Cape of Good Hope the 22nd April Anno 1687, and died here 18 February An. 1737, aged 49 years 9 months and 28 days.

PLATE XXXV.

Hereunder lies buried Classina Adriana Ringers, spouse of the under-merchant, second and fiscal of this Comptoir of Palliacatta, Jacobus Leonardus Topander, born at Flussing, the 12th March Anno 1718, and died here the 9th December A. 1754, being 36 years 8 months and 27 days old.

PLATE XXXVII.

(In Latin)—"Blessed are the dead who die in the Lord." Here lies buried the Honourable, Virtuous, and Upright Lady Petronella Jacoba Leembruggen, deceased spouse of the late Mr. Nicolas Tadama, merchant and chief of the Comptoirs Palliacatta, born at Colombo the

16th Septr. Anno 1753, and fell asleep in the Lord the 4th April Anno 1777 here at Palliacatta, aged 23 years 6 months & 24 days. Having beside her her little son who only was in life for 4 hours after his coming into the world, & of whom she was safely delivered on the 28th October 1776.

CHAPTER XXI.

SADRAS is situated on the sea-shore about 45 miles south of Madras. "It has four villages dependent on it, one of which is an enam held free of rent by a tribe of stone-cutters. The Fort, which was a square building, built of brick, flanked with bastions and contained several useful public buildings was demolished in the year 1781 immediately after its capture. Sadras is stated to have been obtained in A. D. 1612, under agreements entered into with the then Rulers of the Carnatic, and the cession to have been confirmed at the same periods and by the same Native Powers as have been stated under the head of Pulicat with the addition of a Cowle granted by Doud Khan, Nabob of the Carnatic, dated A. D. 1734."[236] The ruins of the houses of the officials of the factory still remain. Inside the fort, is the Dutch cemetery (Pl. XL.), with some old carved tombstones. It is still maintained in order under treaty.[237] These latter date from 1670 to 1790, and are illustrated in plates XLI to LVI. Plates XLIV and XLV are from one slab; the one shows the carving—without the lettering—and pedestal on which the slab rests, and the other gives a fac-simile of the inscription.

CHAPTER XXII.

TANGACHERRY OR TANGASSERI.—A mile north of Quilon. It was captured from the Portuguese in 1665.[238] The possession of this place, enabled the Dutch to command the large expanse of navigable water there entering the sea. The remains of the fort, and a church built during the Dutch occupation in 1789, still exist. The fort is built on a head-land jutting into the sea, and measures about 1 by 2½ furlongs. There are two old cemeteries, with well-carved and inscribed slabs, much weatherworn.[239]

CHAPTER XXIII.

TUTICORIN.—A seaport on the South-east coast, about 324 miles from Madras. It was captured from the Portuguese by the Dutch in 1658.[240]

Tutacoryn—Its dependent Factories, Commercial Lodges and Lascoreen Posts.

"The fort of Tutacoryn is an oblong building standing nearly East and West on the Gulph of Manar. Two sides of it are surrounded by the sea which forms a bason for the admission of Country Boats—Vessels of two or three hundred Tons burthen being obliged to lay without an Island where the Dutch had a yard for the repair of their craft. The fort has bastions at each angle but no glacis or ditch."

"The Government House and buildings within the Fort are in good repair; but the European Houses in the Parawar Town are nearly destroyed—1783."

"The fort and public buildings were demolished in 1805 or 1806."

---

[236] Mad. Govt. Records. *Hodgson's Report. Short Description of the Dutch Settlements*, para. 15.

[237] *Chingpt. Dt. Manl.*, p. 90; *Lists of Antiq.*, p. 189. *Mad. Manl. Admn.* III, p. 775.

[238] *Mad. Manl. Admn.* III, p. 932.

[239] *Lists of Antiq.* p. 260; M.J.L.S., 1879, p. 127; *Mlr.* p. 80.

[240] *Mad. Manl. Admn.* III, p. 933.

"Some of the dependent factories appear also to have been Fortified, all were enclosed with walls. The Warehouses are represented to have been of excellent construction both those on the Coast and Inland.* The Dutch obtained Tutacoryn by conquest from the Portuguese in the year 1658, and appear to have been in great strength at Tutacoryn and on Ceylon about that period. Their claims under this head, it will be seen in the subsequent part of this report, are both of an extent and of a nature seldom heard of for a foreign Nation to possess in a foreign Country, and not claimed by them in any other Province in India. Plans of the Fort of Tutacoryn and of the other factories were transmitted by Mr. Parish to the Board of Revenue, in his letter of the 30th June 1803, & are lodged in the Revenue Office."

* Some of them had been Churches erected by the Portuguese Nation while in possession of Tutacoryn.

"Mr. Irwin in 1783 enumerates the following Factories and Settlements as belonging to the Dutch.[241]

"Keelkarey, 1st, is a factory situated in the Ramnad Country but always dependent on Tutacoryn." "At Kulacurry there is a large Building coming under this discription, which, agreeable to the information I have been able to collect, as mentioned in the accompanying translate of a deposition signed by some Natives of that Place, was in the possession of the Dutch for a period of 37 years to about the year 1795."[242]

"Punnacoil.—The Dutch East India Company received the Madavery † from the Inhabitants, who also allowed the Resident a small gratuity for Fish."

† Madavery is a fee collected for the benefit of the Catholick Churches. See letter from Mr. Cotton, dated 25th February 1818.

"Coilpatam or Johnapatam.—The Resident here received 6 fanams for searching Boats, and for signing Passes for foreign Ditto 1 Pagoda, the Madavery was collected for the Dutch East India Company and the anchorge of Boats at 5 C. fanams each. Every Bale shipped here paid 10½ C. fanams."

"Manapar.—The Dutch East India Company received the Madavery here, and all Bales shipped at Coilpatam paid 10½ C. fanams each, which was divided between the Chief of Tutacoryn and the Chief and Second of Manapar."

"The Inhabitants of Manapar, Dutch, &c., paid something to the Chief for Fish."

"These 'bundle' Customs amounted from 1,500 to 2,000 Chuckrums yearly."

"Cape Comoryn, 2nd.—This factory must long ago have been abandoned, for I can discover no trace of it. N. B.—I have since found that it is situated in the territory of the Rajah of Travancore.

3rd—The agent houses or commercial lodges at Alwar, Tinnevelly, Coilpatam Shaindamungalum and Alundale appear also not to have been occupied since the restitution of Tutacoryn in 1785."

"4th.—The Lascoreen Posts enumerated by the Netherland's Commissioner in his Claims were ports or posts occupied to secure their monopoly of all Cloth manufactured in Tinnevelly to aid the searching of all vessels navigating the Gulf of Manar to compel the owners to take out a Dutch pass, and pay the fee for it, and to collect the other fees enumerated by Mr Irwin."[243] Fryer mentions the place, under the name Tutticaree.[244] He did not, however, land there, as the Dutch and English were then at war.[245] The Church

---

241 Mad. Govt. Records. *Hodgson's Report. Short Description of the Dutch Settlements*, paras. 19–23.

242 Letter from the Commercial Resident at Ramnad to the Government of Fort St. George, dated 17th April 1817.

243 Mad. Govt. Records. *Hodgson's Report. Short Description of the Dutch Settlements*, para. 23.

244 Travels 1672–3, p. 49.

245 *Lists of Antiq.*, p. 308.

at present used for worship, was erected by the Dutch in 1750.[246] There is a Dutch obelisk lighthouse.[247]

The place is still an important seaport. It is the southern terminus of the South Indian Railway. There is an old cemetery (plate LVII), with some elaborately carved Dutch tombstones. Examples dating from 1810 to 1824 are given in plates LVIII to LXII. Plates LVIII and LIX are respectively the carving and lettering of one slab. Plate LXI is a lofty obelisk, built of brick, and moulded in stucco. There is an inscription on the upper square; it is shown on plate LXII.

CHAPTER XXIV.

A TRADITIONAL DUTCH COLONY ON THE NELLORE COAST.

Juvuladinne stands on the coast, at the mouth of the Chippaleru river, 24 miles north-north-east of Nellore and 62 miles north of Armegam, where the English East India Company had a settlement in 1628.

The modern village stands to the west of an extensive mound—now covered with drift sand, and under cultivation—after which it is named. The local account of the origin of 'Juvuladinne' is, that it is derived from a plant *juvul*, which once covered the mound, but there is no such similar term in the very complete list of the flora of the district given in the district manual,[248] and it seems improbable that this is the correct explanation. The adjacent remains show it to have been an ancient site; one of the many seaports which, prior to or during the period of the decay and fall of Buddhism, from the fourth to the eighth centuries, seem to have existed along this coast; though now, as is general with them, through the recession of the coast line seawards, it stands at some distance inland. In all of those which I have visited, there is a tradition of their having been destroyed by an inundation of the sea. This may have been so, more especially as the tradition is so general. The towns being thus either partially or completely destroyed, would not again to any extent revive, though some might carry on a lingering existence.

About a mile south by east of the village, a quarter of a mile distant from the coast line, and on the south of a salt marsh, once traditionally an arm of the sea, is an extensive mound. It rises with a somewhat steep slope to a height of about 15 feet direct from the edge of the waterline of the marsh. The surface of the mound is nearly level, and forms almost a square with sides of about 60 yards in length. The angles are rounded off, as by bastions, and stand at the cardinal points of the compass; the faces being at the intermediate points. Broken bricks are strewn over the surface of the north-west side, which has less drift sand than the others. Beyond this mound, to the south, the ground is broken by a number of smaller ones now covered by sand. The large mound is supposed to be the site of a fort, and is named Gudikurtikota. It is also known, after the European settlers whom local tradition states to have built it as Uland or Wallandulakota, that is, the fort of the Hollanders. Vallandupalem—Holland palem—is the name applied to the site in Masulipatam where the Dutch had their villa residences.[249]

---

[246] *Tinvlly. Dt. Manl.*, pp. 60–61. [247] *Mad. Manl. Admn.* III, p. 933. [248] *Nlr. Dt. Manl.*, pp. 95–145. [249] *Kist. Dt. Manl.*, p. 100.

During my visit to the place, I was unable to spare time for any extensive digging, but, as no walls were visible on the surface, a slight excavation was necessary to determine whether any really did exist. On the north-west side, three trenches were dug at 12 feet apart. They proved the ground to consist of red sandy soil for a depth of 4 feet, with yellow sea sand below. The trenches were carried in just below the point where the ground dips down from the upper level, as, should walls exist, it was to be expected from the configuration of the ground, they would be found there. The west trench exposed a wall, 3 feet thick, running north and south. Running parallel to it, at a foot distant, was another of similar breadth. They were traced for a length of 12 feet. The middle trench cut into a large deposit of oyster shells mixed with broken bricks. The east touched a wall running east and west. The bricks forming these walls are of large size, and such as are only found in very early buildings. They measure $20'' \times 9\frac{3}{4}'' \times 2\frac{1}{2}''$. The bricks were laid on blocks of stone, and could not from their position, nature, and plan, be those of the fort. Such bricks are not found in early European buildings in the south, nor were they used in later Indian works. The uncovered walls doubtless represent some building which had existed there before the fort was erected.

Extensive digging in the drift sand would be necessary, to lay bare the plan, and the nature of the construction of the fort. It is probable, that if it were constructed of brick, its isolated position after desertion, would lead to its being used as a quarry by the surrounding villages; and it is thus doubtful if much or any of the material may now remain.

Tradition only retained the name, but was silent as to the date and duration of the settlement. Such traditions, however, have usually some foundation on fact. If it had been in existence for any considerable period, doubtless some of the carved tombstones, usually found at Dutch sites, might still exist buried under the sand; or, probably, being in such a remote position, they may have gone the way of the fort itself. In others of their settlements, situated near towns or considerable villages, the tombstones were, and are still carefully preserved. [250]

---

[250] G.O., No. 382, Public, dated 30th April 1889, pp. 2–5.

PART III.—INDO-DUTCH COINAGE.

CHAPTER XXV.

RECORDS RELATING TO MINTAGE.

The earliest money brought by the Dutch to India, to exchange for eastern commodities, would doubtless be European, of the kinds made current by their predecessors, the Portuguese and others.

After they had secured a certain footing in the country, they opened mints, where gold, silver and copper were coined. Mints are known to have existed at Bimlipatam, Pulicat, Jaganadhapuram, Negapatam, Galle, Batavia; and certain places whose coins bear the mint initial letter C and T, being probably either Colombo or Cochin, and Trincomalee, Tuticorin or Tegnapatam. There may have been other mints, but from these places at any rate, money was supplied to their other stations. They seem to have had the right of coinage at all their stations; but it is doubtful if it was exercised at others than those named. The distinguishing feature of their coins, is the company's monogram on the obverse, a large V, with the smaller lettering O.C. placed on its arms. (Vereenigde Oost—Indisch compagnie,—United East Indian Company. See Pls. XIX, XXI, LXIII.) Records, before quoted, refer to their having, in 1679, landed at Masulipatam, a large stock of copper and silver, and also gold, which had been recently coined at Pulicat. A large amount of money too, was sent there from Batavia, to carry on the cloth trade. In Gódávari, prior to 1787, a lakh of Madras pagodas had been annually imported for a similar purpose. Their gold coins approximated to the first European ducats introduced by the Venetians, which still continued to be highly valued. Their indigenous copper coinage resembles, perhaps not unintentionally, the primitive tokens of the native powers, among whom they were settled.

Latterly, supplies of superior qualities of silver and copper coin, seem to have been minted in Europe, and sent out for use in the colonies. These did not altogether displace the produce of the Indian mints, which still continued the issue of money.

There are signs of the Netherlands East India company having been confronted with an incipient exchange problem; but the evidences go to prove that they turned it to their own advantage.

The matter is mentioned by Canter Visscher (1743); and the following extract from the Madras Records, bears on a local phase of the same subject:—

"Pub. 101. Fort St. George, October 1679.

At a Consultation.

Thursday, the 16th.

Present:

"Mr. Joseph Hynmers, Deputy Governour, Mr. John Bridger, Mr. Timothy Wilkes.

Whereas the Governour of Palliacatt, hath three severall times by beate of Drum forbidden the People there to receive our great Copper Cash, because they passe at 42 for one fanam of this Place, and their Cash being of the same weight that ours is, of which they give there but 45 for one fanam of Palliacatt which is $1\frac{1}{4}$ fanam of

This town Inhabitants forbidden to receive Palliacat Cash.

Madras, and consequently our fanam amounts there but to 36 Palliacat Cash, and we give 42 of our Cash, which is the same weight with the Palliacat Cash, It is hereby enordered that the Inhabitants of this place, be by beate of Drum 3 severall dayes forbidden to receive the Palliacat Cash.

JOSEPH HYNMERS.
J. W. BRIDGER.
TIMO. WILKES."

Some information, regarding the coinage and mints, is found in the accompanying extract from the records of Fort St. George.

Hodgson's report.

" Mint.

" Coinage of copper, silver and gold.

66. The Commissioner on the part of His Majesty's the King of the Netherlands claims a right to re-establish a Mint and to coin Copper, Silver and Gold coins at Bimlipatam (*a*) Jagganautpooram (*b*) Pulicat and Tutacoryn.

(*a*) It appears that the Dutch coined copper at Bimlipatam up to A. D. 1794. The cowles of the Rajah of Vizianagaram, copies of which have been received from the Collector of Vizagapatam, since the report was prepared, mention the mint as one of the privileges granted.

(*b*) The silver coins issued by the Dutch at Bimlipatam were coined at Jagganautpooram.

" 67.—From the information I have been able to collect from a perusal of the records for a considerable period back, and, from a reference to documents of ancient date, I have reason to be satisfied that the Dutch East India Company actually possessed a Mint at Pulicat—at Jagganautpooram, at Bimlipatam and at Tutacoryn. If the right of coinage be however a sovereign right, the Dutch East India Company holding Bimlipatam under a grant from the Rajah of Vizianagarum only, himself a tributary of the Emperors of Delhi or of the Nizam could not, by virtue of the grant of the Rajah, claim the right of coinage at Bimlipatam. But as the right has been exercised without being questioned by the British Government for a long period antecedent and subsequent to the grant of the Circars to the Company and as the exercise of it does not appear to me calculated to injure the interests of the Hon'ble the East India Company I have no objection to offer to an admission of the right.

The Nizam is stated to have confirmed the grant in A.D. 1628.

" 68. Should the Dutch resume the Coinage of Copper coin, these coins will only be current according to the current price of Copper. Experience in India has established the fact that coins cannot be made to circulate at a rate different from the current value of the metal of which they are composed, except in cases where an undue preference is given to any particular coin by the receivers of the public revenue. This fact has been amply illustrated in the issue and receipt of the Copper coins received by this Government at different times from England.

" 69. Should the Coinage of Silver and Gold be resumed either at Bimlipatam, Jagganautpooram Pulicat, or Tutacoryn, and the coins issued from those mints prove defective or too much alloyed, the circulation of such description of coins will be easily prevented by the British Government forbidding their receipt in payment of the public revenue. The expense of keeping up a mint establishment is not however likely to be repaid by any seignorage, it may be practicable for the Dutch authorities to buy on a currency of restricted circulation.

" 70. It does not appear that the Dutch have had a Mint at work at Pulicat for near a century, and this information supplied by Mr. Grāeme is confirmed by the non-existence in circulation of any coins coined more recently at Pulicat. Mr. Grāeme has furnished me with specimens of the half gold, half silver fanam and of the copper cash once coined at that place, but states that the Pulicat pagoda has gone out of use.

" 71. I have received a specimen of the Dutch Cominghy, *i.e.*, Company's Pagoda coined at Tutacoryn which is represented to be of a higher value than the Star Pagoda by 3 or 4 per cent.

" 72. Mr. Irwin in 1783 reported that the Dutch coined annually at Tutacoryn near two lacs of Cominghy Pagodas and also 5 Lacs of gold fanams. The revenue they derived from the Mint yielded about 7,700 Star Pag[s], and many instruments used in coining were given up when Tutacoryn was captured.

"73. Under all the circumstances exemplified in this report relating to the revenues of the Dutch possessions on tho coast of Coromandel, it is not to be expected that the Dutch will ever re-establish a Mint for the ooinage of Silver or Gold, altho' it may occasionally answer their purpose to eoin eopper coins.

"74. It will be for the Governor in Council to determine whether the right of coinage is one of the rights abandoned on the part of His Majesty the King of the Netherlands by the IV article of the convention of the 13th August 1814 under the interpretation put on that article respecting the exemption from Duties and Customs by the orders of the Honorable Court of Directors of the 7th November 1814. If all right of sovereignty claimed by the Dutch nation in the Settlements situated within the sovereignty of the British Government have been abandoned by that article, it would follow that the right of establishing and working a Mint had been also abandoned equally with the right of an exemption from duties—whether the right to a Mint has been given up or remains in full force, it would be desirable perhaps in any new negotiation to stipulate for the relinquishment of the privilege,—a privilege now of little value to the Dutch, but one which may occasionally be productive of inconvenience to the British administration." [251]

The coins current in 1743, are described by Canter Visscher, a Dutch chaplain of Cochin. A French extract appears in the M.J.L.S., 1887–88, pp. 184–85. The following is a translation of the portions relating to Dutch coinage.

"European money was—in silver—écus named risdales, ducatons, Spanish piastres called Spaansche matten: in gold—ducats;—and finally in copper—dutes and demi-dutes.

The East India Company have adopted the florin as a standard, notwithstanding that the risdale is in Europe equivalont to 50 sous, and in the Indies only to 48 sous, it is generally employed in commercial and private transactions

The ducaton was the money principally put in circulation by the Company, but chiefly at Batavia. Its value was fixed by the Company's tarif at 13 escalins or schellingen of 6 sous while in reality it was not worth more than 10½ escalins.

In this way the Company made a profit of 2½ escalins, that is 15 sous upon each ducaton.

Ducats were principally used in the trado with Persia. Tho Netherlands establishments at Malabar and Ceylon were generally supplied with ducats since the pepper trade was carried on with this money in gold fixed at the rate of 18 escalins. Venetian ducats were most valued.

The small coins in lead or copper were named boes ero kken and cas or cashs. Pagodas were of the same weight as ducats, and were valued at two risdales. Rupees and half rupees in gold and silver were also in circulation throughout India."

With the aid of the particulars given above, and some others marginally noted, the following provisional table of coins and their relative values may be prepared :—

Standard=Florin (gold).
5 oash (copper)=1 demi dute, or duit (copper).
10 cash (copper)=1 dute (copper).[252]
20 cash (copper)=1 stuiver (copper). 1 and 2 stuiver copper and silver coins.
4 stuivers=1 fanam (gold and silver).[253]
12 fanams=1 rix dollar.[254]
6 sous or stuivers (copper)=1 escalin or schelling (silver).
A 30 stuiver silver coin (name ?).[255]

---

[251] Mad. Govt. Records. *Hadgson's Report—Short Description of the Dutch Settlements*, paras. 66 to 74.

[252] See *Mad. Manl. Admn.*, p. 616, where it is stated that 10 cash were equal to 1 doody (dût or dûd) and 8 doodies equal to 1 silver fanam.

[253] M.M.C.C., No. 268, see also below, where 80 cash aro noted as equal to a fanam.

[254] "Cinamon is invoiced as well to Europe as every part of India at 25 Rix Dollars per Balo. The terms on which thoy procure the cinamon are thoso; every man is allowed 7½ fanams (of which there are 12 to a Rix Dollar)" *Military Sundry Book* 1762, No 17. *Mr. Pybus' mission to Kandy.*

[255] M.J.L.S., 1887–8, p. 184. See succeeding article "silver coins."

48 stuivers = 1 rix dollar or ryx daler (silver) [256] and
48 or 50 sous (or stuivers) = 1 écu or risdalé (silver).[256]
$10\frac{1}{2}$ or 13 escalins (and 80 stuivers) = 1 ducaton or dukaton (silver),
(63, 78 and 80 stuivers.). [257]
2 risdalés or rix dollars = 1 ducat or dukaat.
(96 or 100 stuivers) (gold) also
18 escalins.
(108 stuivers) = 1 ducat.[258]

The following was the value of the copper cash (weight about 7 to 10 grains) relative to other coins in circulation. The Dutch and English coins were of the same weight. The value seems to have varied at different periods. Thus in 1679, from 36 to 45 cash went to a fanam.[259]

" Munday 22nd . . . . . 'Tis ordered that Captain Knox Bill of Exchange be paid according to the terms drawn upon us by ye Worsp^ll^ Charless ffleetwood Deputy Govern^r^, &c., Councell of ye West coast ye A^mot^ being 1300 : Dollars at ye usall Interest from May last terms very reason^ble^ and well aproved off, as also £ 10 on acco^t^ Mr. Charles ffriths sallary he owing soe much to y^e^ Capt. as by their letter and desire.

Mr. Stone Assay Master reported y^e^ Assayes of the Pagoda and fan^m^ last rec^d^ from Fort St. David as ℘ their Generalltre: dated y^e^ 10th Instant vizt: the fanams $3\frac{1}{2}$ matt, & the Palliacatt pagoda $8\frac{5}{8}$ matt wch is according to standard but y^e^ fanams worse $\frac{3}{4}$ matt wch is about 18 ℘ ^ct^. most abominable Cheat.

E. LIHU YALE.
NAT HIGGINSON.
WILL : FRASER."[260]

Previous to 1846, Madras Government dues were paid at the rate of 80 cash to a fanam ; and 42, 44 or 45 fanams to a star pagoda.[261]

The Porto Novo pagoda weighed about $17\frac{1}{4}$ carats or ·720 fine. In exchange, 120 of them were valued at 100 star pagodas. In Government accounts, 36 fanams went to the Porto Novo pagoda, and $37\frac{1}{2}$ in the bazaar.[262]

Coins are yet found in considerable number on the sites of the settlements ; and some are often seen among old coins purchasable in the towns of Southern India, whence they have found their way in offerings to the temples. On the sites, they are picked up after the surface of the ground has been disturbed by rain. The majority are Dutch copper coins. Others are of different East India Companies ; and some foreign coins sometimes appear among them.

---

256 An English Ceylonese silver coin (weighing 140 grains) was of 48 stuivers value, and equal to the rix dollar. In the English issue of coinage in Ceylon at the beginning of present century, are a number of pieces, doubtless a continuation of others made current by the Dutch. They include coins of 24, 48 and 96 stuivers value in silver, and others of $\frac{1}{4}$, $\frac{1}{2}$, 1, 2 and 4 stuivers in copper. (M.M.C.C., No. 2, 68.)

The risdale (assumably rix-dollar) was worth 48 sous (see above). It is obvious from the coincidence, that the terms sou and stuiver were then equivalent, and that the risdale and rix dollar were one coin. (See remarks in next article.) I do not overlook the fact of the present values of the sou and the modern Dutch stuiver, and that about 48 of the former go to a ryx daler ; but we know that copper money has steadily decreased in weight and relative value.

257 Proceedings of a Committee assembled at Colombo, August 1797.

258 From the paragraph from which this is quoted, it appears that this rate was fixed for certain transactions which were entirely carried on in gold ; and in which the Dutch would have to pay money for articles received. The arbitrary enhancement of its value would enable them to make a profit of from 8 to 12 stuivers on every ducat they paid.

259 Public records, October 1679, p. 101.

260 Public consultations 1692. General No. 18. Fort St. George. August 1692, p. 121.

261 *Chingpt. Dt. Manl.* p. 59.

262 *Mad. Manl. Admn.*, p. 616.

CHAPTER XXVI.

GOLD COINAGE.

European coins of the period, in this metal, are extremely rare. Most of them have probably been melted down, and converted into jewellery. Some have been preserved strung on necklaces.

The Venetian ducat (zeccino or sequin) was at one time current, and is sometimes met with. It is a thin coin, weighing from 51 to 54 grains, and in diameter measuring 0·85 inch. This is almost exactly the size of the copper challis. On the obverse, is the Saviour in aureole, surrounded by the contracted legend.

SIT. T. XTE. DAT. Q. TV. REGIS. ISTE. DVCA.

(*sit tibi, Christe datus, quem tu regis, iste Ducatus.*)

On the reverse is St. Peter (or St. Mark ?) delivering the ivory sceptre, surmounted by a cross, to the kneeling Doge. The surrounding legend contains the name of the Doge Aloi Mocen.

S. M. VENET. DVX. ALOI. MOCEN. (PL. LXIII figs. 1, 2).

Another gold coin of the same size as the sequin, is illustrated in figs. 3, 4. It is of the time of William V. of the Netherlands, and may be a memorial coin or token. On the obverse is a mail clad warrior, with a sword in the right hand and a sheaf of arrows in the left. Around is the legend CONCORDIA. RBS. PAR. CP. BS. HOL., and the date 1776. On the reverse is a square in floral devices, with the inscription MO. ORD. PROVIN FOEDER BELGAD LEG. IMP.

CHAPTER XXVII.

SILVER COINAGE.

EARLY coins in this metal are scarce. A coin, of which it has been stated only a very few were struck, and which is now but seldom met with, was the rix dollar. [263] The statement as to there having been but a small issue of rix dollars, is a negative assumption deduced from the fact of their present scarcity. It would seem to require some remarks, in view of the fact, stated in the previous article, that the écu (crown) 'named risdale' was the medium usually 'employed in commercial and private transactions.' The word 'dollar' is a corruption of the Low German 'dăller' and Danish 'dăler,' and hence the contraction 'dăle.' Rix dollar would thus seem to be a corruption of 'rux-dăler' or 'risdălé,' and be the actual coin noted under the latter name in the article referred to. The modern Dutch equivalent is rijksdaalder. It is mentioned distinct from the Spanish piastre or dollar, then also in circulation. The florin—equal to the gulden or—guilder, was the *unite de compte*. The early florin was a gold coin of the size of a ducat. It was first struck at Florence in the thirteenth century. It, I presume, was the standard referred to. The silver florin is a modern coin.

Government records also show, that the rix-dollar was the common currency of Ceylon; and when this is so, it is difficult to credit the assumption that only a few could have been struck.

---

[263] M.J.L.S., 1887-88, p. 184; M.M.C.C. No. 2., p. 67.

"The necessary Examination of Papers for a detailed Investigation of the Revenues of Ceylon has required much time and attention, as the Books of this Island in common with those of the other Dutch Colonies appear to have had for their object only such a Register of the Transactions of the Colonial Government as might enable the Book-keepers in Europe to draw a general Balance of the affairs of the Company, the state of which was entirely unknown to their servants abroad, and to facilitate the labour of the European offices, the accounts of all the colonies are kept in Dutch Guilders. No part of the Receipts and Issues of the Revenue of Ceylon being made in this coin. I have in all the Documents to which I shall refer converted Guilders to Rix Dollars equal to Rupees, the Currency of the Country ; this besides the advantage of being more clear to the Comprehension of Government, renders it unecessary to touch on the variations of Exchange which would embarass our Investigation with long and intricate calculations."[264] Calculations of matters relating to revenue are in the first of the proceedings above quoted, stated in rix-dollars, fanams stuivers and cashs. The equivalent in ducatoons is also given. Forty-eight stuivers went to a rix-dollar and eighty to a ducatoon. Latterly the totals are also entered in star pagodas.

There were a number of silver coins of various denominations, such as the 30 stuiver piece and others. Six-stuiver pieces (escalins or schellingen ?) have a ship on the obverse, sometimes surrounded by the inscription 'In Deo est spes nostra ;' and with the coat-of-arms of the state, crown, date and value on the reverse.

The small coins of one and two stuivers value, dating from the latter period of the Dutch occupation, are most common. Some of Frisia are found with the date 1660. They have emblems similar to those described in a succeeding article on the copper challis.

CHAPTER XXVIII.

INDIAN COPPER COINAGE.

PLATE LXIII.

In the stuiver series of Indian mintage, there is as great variety in the weight of coins of any one denomination, as there is in their forms. It would almost seem as if some metal had been poured out at hazard, in quantity approximating to what was considered necessary, and then hurriedly impressed, either with the whole or any portion of the stamp. A great deal of the difference, but not all, may be due to wear and tear of the coins, and, perhaps some, to varying weights at the several mints. As to their outline, it would indeed be matter of difficulty to find any two alike. They are simply shapeless pieces of flattened metal, less symmetrical than many of the purely Indian coins which they imitate.

Among the earliest issues of the Indian minted stuivers, are coins of 2, 1, $\frac{1}{2}$, $\frac{1}{4}$ and $\frac{1}{8}$ values. The term duit, or dute, has sometimes been used concurrently with stuiver ; but it would seem that it should be more properly restricted only to the fractional values of the stuiver. They are thick and roughly made, and of irregular form, the dies having little reference in their size to that of the coin. On the obverse is the Company's monogram V.O.C. The abbreviation S. T. is used for stuiver.

A later form of stuiver, sometimes un-dated, but usually bearing dates extending from 1784 to 1795, was also struck at the Indian mints, and exhibits similar irregularity

264 No. 25, R. D. Proceedings of a Committee of Investigation assembled at Colombo, 4th August 1797, p. 165, Sundry.

in form. On the obverse is the monogram V.O.C., and initial of mint place : on the reverse is the value. Those with the letter C, have the word " stuiver " and date below.

Figures 5, 6. Copper. Round. It bears no mark of value but is probably a two-stuiver piece, though it now only weighs about a half more than the one-stuiver pieces Nos. 7–8 and 11–12. Weight 300 grains.

Obverse.—Monogram V.O.C. with initial letter G (Galle) over. Below are two squares of four dots each, and two circular figures. A border of dots encircles a half of the coin. On the other half it is away.

Reverse.—Date 1789, with a square of four dots over. The dotted border appears on a portion of the circumference, ending in two scrolls under the date.

Figures 7, 8. Copper stuiver. Irregular round. Weight 206 grains.

Obverse.—Monogram V.O.C. surmounted by letter C (Colombo or Cochin).

Reverse.—Figure I between two squares of four dots.

STUIVE over date 1795, and portion of dotted border under.

Figures 9, 10. Copper stuiver. Irregular round. Weight 192 grains.

Obverse.—Portion of monogram V.O.C. with letter T (Tegnapatam or Trincomalee ?) above.

Reverse.—Abbreviation S.T., for stuiver, separated by two lines from date 179 (9 or 2 ?) below.

Figures 11, 12. A specimen of Nos. 7–8, weighing 207 grains. The shape varies, and the figure I and dotted rim do not show on the reverse. Date 1795. The figure 7 appears as a 2.

Figures 13, 14. Copper stuiver. Irregular round. Weight 191 grains.

Obverse.—Monogram V.O.C. and portion of mint-place initial C (Colombo or Cochin ?).

Reverse.—Figure I between two squares of four dots. STUIVI with three figures of date 17 (0 or 9 ?) below.

Figures 5 to 14 are from casts of coins in the Madras Museum.

Figures 15, 16. A copper demi-duit ; round : no marked date or value. Weight 24 grains. According to the foregoing table of coinage, there are eight demi-dutes in a stuiver. This coin weighs an eighth of No. 9–10. On the obverse is the monogram V.O.C., surmounted by P (Pulicat) : the rim marked with dots. The reverse has two semi-circular figures—one with a dot, and the other with a triangle ; enclosed with a ring of dots. Figures 17–18 show a similar coin, differing chiefly in the reversal of the letter P.

Another coin has on the obverse the monogram V.O.C., with the letter N either right or reversed. On the reverse is the word Nagapattanam (Negapatam) in Tamil or Grantha. Examples are figures 20 to 25.

Figure 27 is a small coin, with the monogram enclosed by two plain concentric circles on the obverse. On the reverse is a small dotted circle surrounded by some illegible letters. There is nothing to show the place of mintage.

A curious piece of money is mentioned as having been found in Ceylon.[265] It is described as a small bar of metal " about the size of one's little finger," having both ends flattened out ; with the company's monogram at one end, and the value $4\frac{1}{2}$ S. T. at the other.

---

[265] M.J.L.S., 1887–88, p. 182.

CHAPTER XXVII.

EUROPEAN COPPER COINAGE.

A CLASS of coin, which is even yet commonly met with, at the sites of the old Dutch settlements on the continent of Southern India, and in Ceylon, is the Challi, also named dutc or duit. They are still current in Cochin. They are thin and well stamped coins. The superiority of their make, has led to the inference, that they were struck in Holland, and sent out for circulation in the Dutch eastern settlements. They are mostly of $\frac{1}{4}$ or $\frac{1}{2}$ stuiver value. The latter has $\frac{1}{2}$ S.T. over the monogram. On the obverse is the company's monogram, with the mint mark above, varying in figure according to the date. Below is the date, said to range from 1726 to 1798. I have, however,—in a large and widely obtained collection—found none earlier than 1730, or later than 1792. Some coins also bear the name of the State, as Zeelandia, &c. On the reverse is a coat-of-arms, surmounted by a crown. On one class of coin, there occurs on the reverse, one of the names—Java-Indiæ, Batav, or Nederl-Indie, with the date under. The reverse is the chief distinguishing feature in their designs, and is varied according to the State represented.

Friesland or Vriesland (Frisia).—The shield charged with two lions passant gardant. Dates 1731 to 1792.

Coins of the following dates have been collected: 1732–33–35–36–37; 1744–45–46–48; 1750–51–53–54–55–56; 1765–66; 1772; 1780–81–87; 1791–92. 1732 has a bulged-pointed shield; on the others it is square. The mint mark on 1730 is a lily and five-petalled flower on each side. In the forties and fifties it is a cock with a dot on each side: the sixties and seventies have a boat (?) with the same dots; the eighties and nineties have a five-petalled flower with dots. (Figures 28 to 30.)

Guelders (Gelderland).—Shield, party per pale, charged with two lions rampant combatant, with inscription around. In the dates 1731–32 it is the contracted " In Deo S.P. Nos." : in the others " In Deo est spes nostra." There are coins of 1731–32; 1786–87–88–89; 1790–91–92. 1731 has a mint mark of a horse and two dots; 1732 a line with small circles over and two dots; 1786 a bud with two spikes on each side, between two five-petalled flowers: 1790 is the same as 1786, but between two stars. (Figures 31 to 33.)

Holland.—Shield charged with a rampant lion facing right. Dates noted are—1730–31–32–34–35–36–37; 1743–44–45–46–47–48–49; 1750–51–52–53–57; 1766–68; 1780–84; 1790. All have a mint mark of a five-leaved flower between two dots. (Figures 34 to 37.)

Utrecht.—A shield, party per bend, supported by two lions rampant. The smaller coins want the supporters. Dates are—1744–45–46; 1752–53–54–55–57; 1766; 1776–77; 1780–81–84–86–87–88–89; 1790–91–92. All, except 1790, have a shield for mint mark, with dot on each side; the exception has a star. All the specimens of 1790 found, have been defaced. (Figures 38 to 43.)

Zeeland.—The shield charged with a demi-lion rampant, and three wavy lines fess-wise. Field of the coin is sometimes inscribed with " Luctor et emergo" around. Dates noted are—1731 to 39; 1744 to 49; 1750–52–53–54–56–57; 1765; 1779; 1785–86–88–89; 1790–91–92. The mint mark on the first three decades is a large castle between two stars; the others have a small castle. (Figures 44, 45.)

INDEX.

A

B

C

D

E

F

G

H

I

J

N

O

P

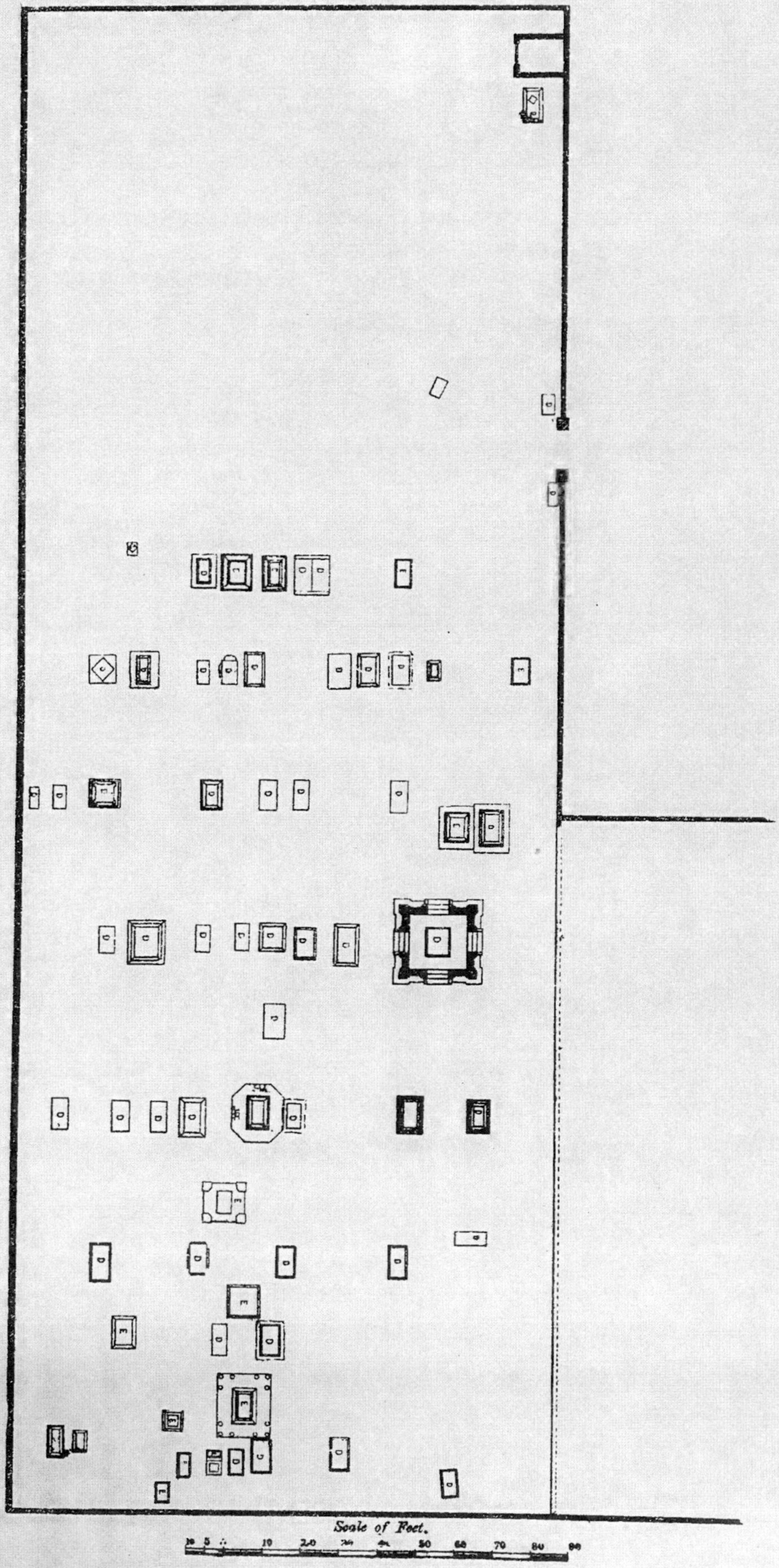

Photo., S. I. O., Calcutta.

Scale ⅛th of Original.

Photo., S. I. O., Calcutta.

Photo., S. I. O., Calcutta.

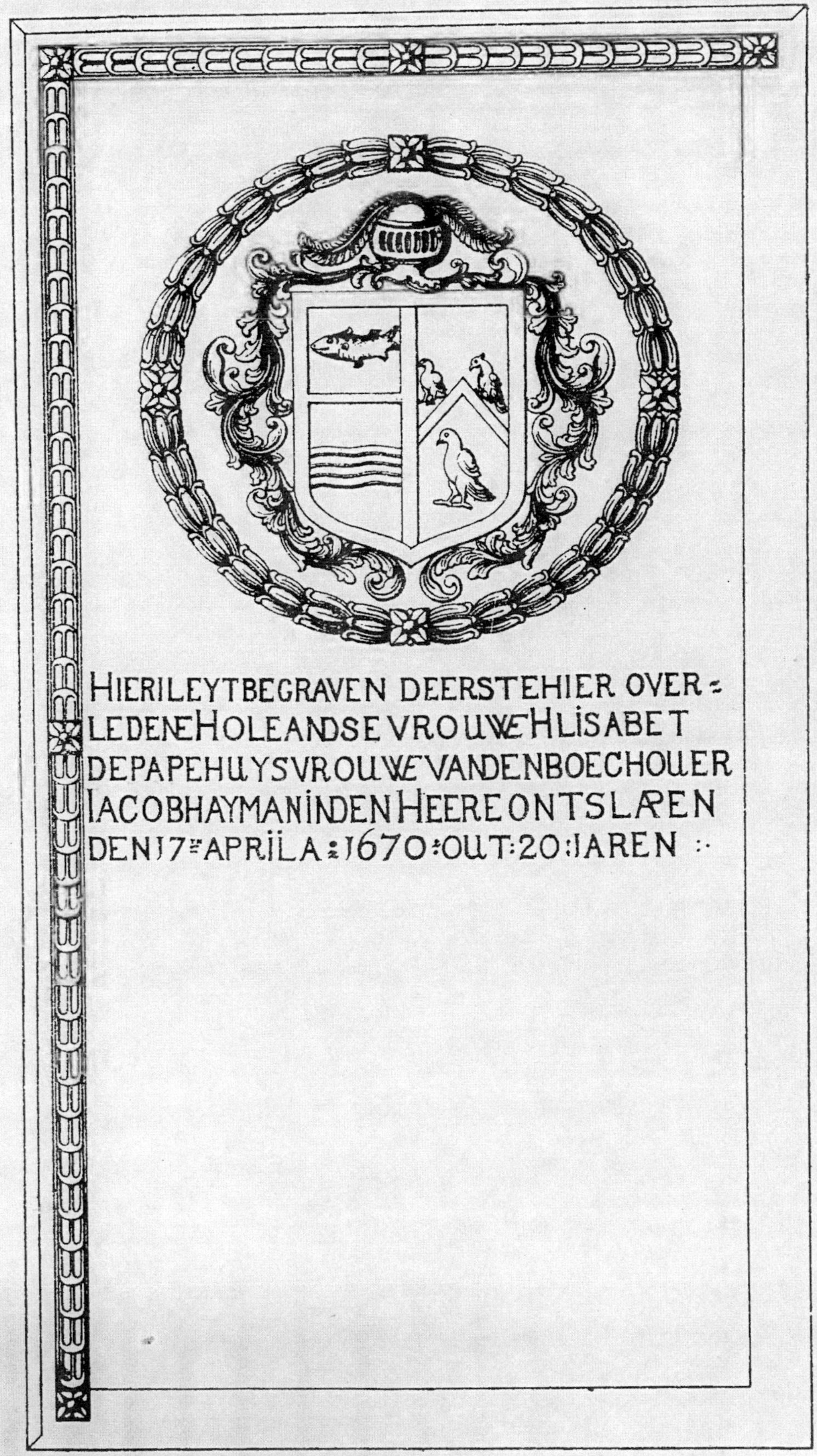

Scale of Feet.

12 6 0 1 2 3 4

Photo. S. I. O., Calcutta.

Scale ⅛th of Original.

Photo., S. I. O., Calcutta.

Scale ⅛th of Original.

Photo. S. I. O., Calcutta.

Scale of Feet.

12 6 0 1 2 3

Photo., S. I. O., Calcutta

Scale ⅛th of Original.

Photo. S. I. O., Calcutta.

HODIE MIHI CRAS TIBI
HIER ONDER LEYD BEGRAVIEN
DEN WELED CEBOREN HEER
HENDRIK DU BON
INSYNED: LEVEN OPPERCOOPMAN,
HOOFDAMINISTRATEUR EN TWEF=
DE VAN DE CUST CORMANDEL
GEBOOREN TE MIDDEBURG IN ZEE=
LAND. DEN 23: DECEMBER A: 1718 EN
OVERLEEDEN TE NAGAPATNAM
DEN 23: IUNY A: 1753
OUD
34. IAAREN EN 6 MAANDEN
Scale of Feet.
12 6 0 1 2 3 4 5

Scale ⅛th of Original.

Photo., S. I. O., Calcutta.

Scale ⅛th of Original

Photo. S. I. O., Calcutta.

Scale ⅓th of Original.

Photo. S. I. O., Calcutta.

Scale ⅓th of Original.

Photo., S. I. O., Calcutta.

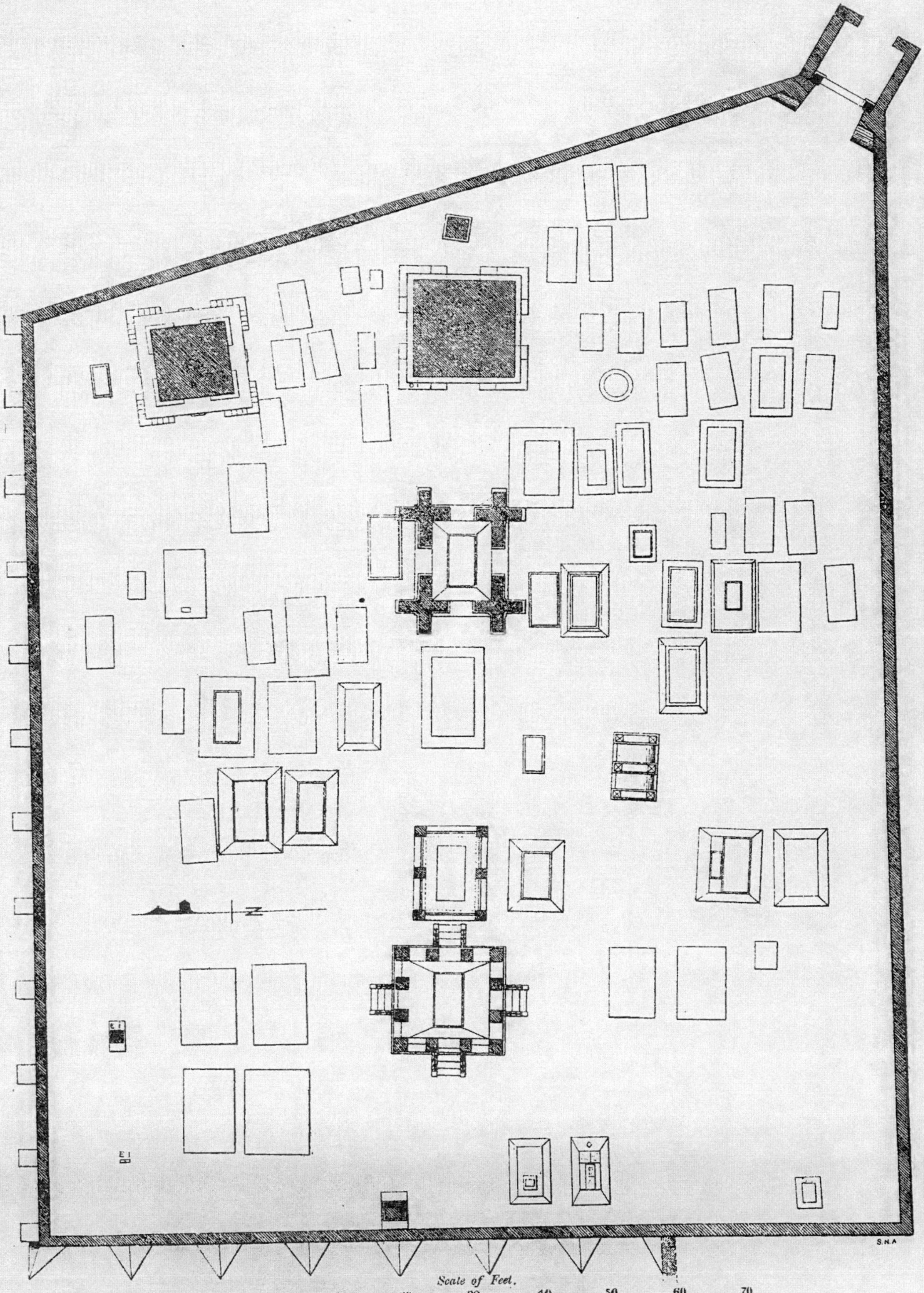

Photo., S. I. O., Calcutta.

Photo. S. I. O., Calcutta.

Photo. S. I. O., Calcutta

Scale ⅛th of Original.

Photo., S. I. O., Calcutta.

Photo. S. I. O., Calcutta.

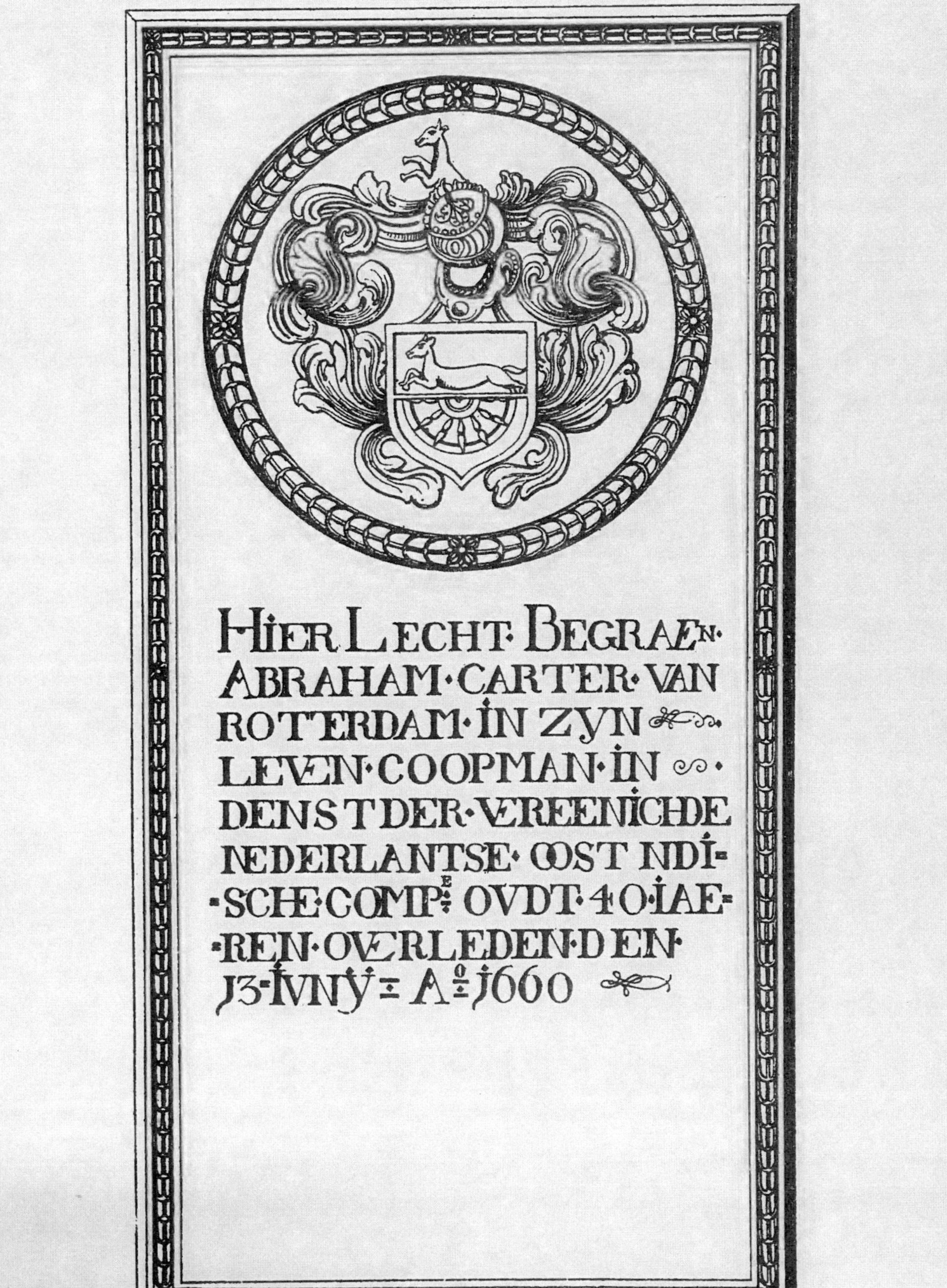

Scale of Feet.

Photo., S. I. O., Calcutta

Scale [illegible]th of Original.

Photo. S. I. O., Calcutta.

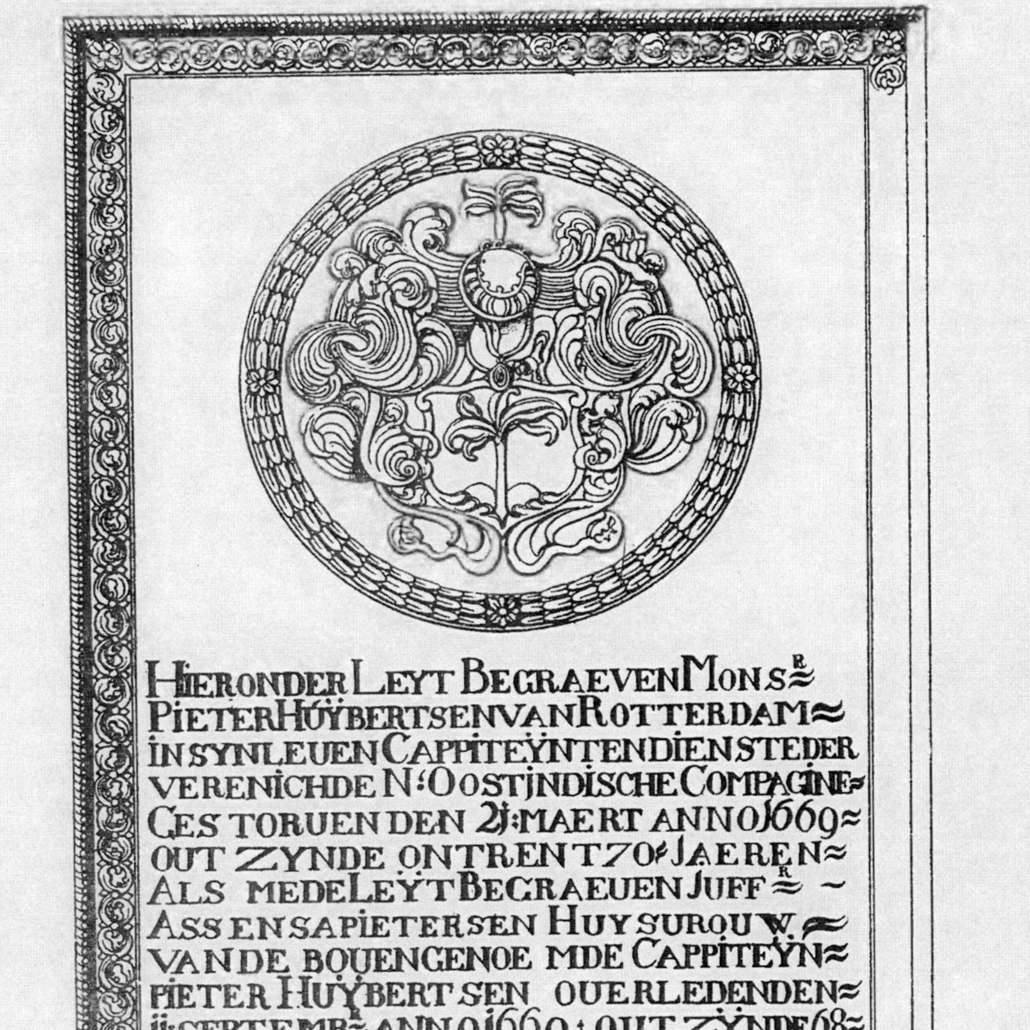

Scale of Feet.

Photo. S. I. O., Calcutta.

Scale of Feet.

Photo., S. I. O., Calcutta.

Scale of Feet.

Photo., S. I. O., Calcutta

Scale of Feet.

Photo. S. I. O., Calcutta.

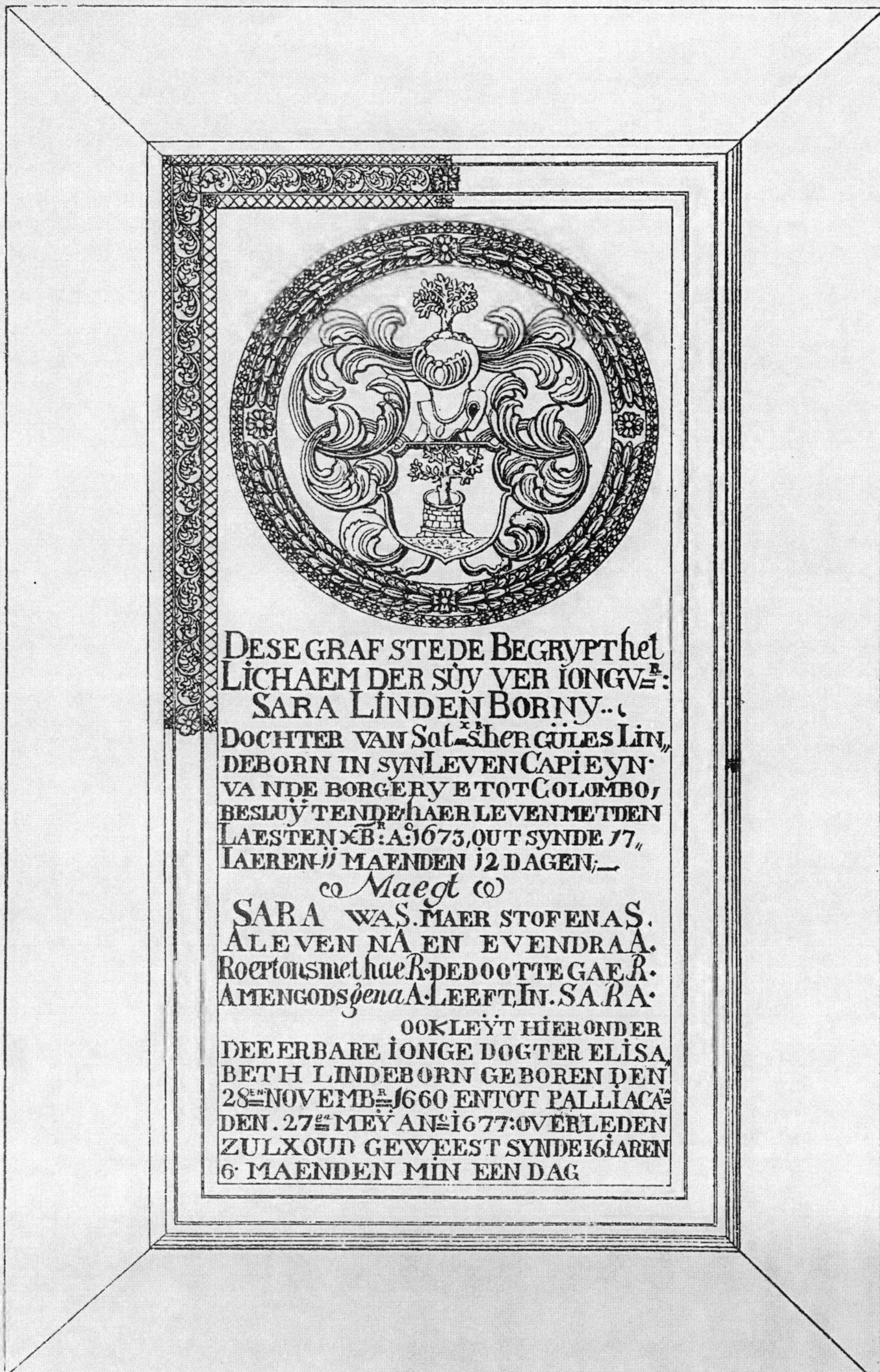

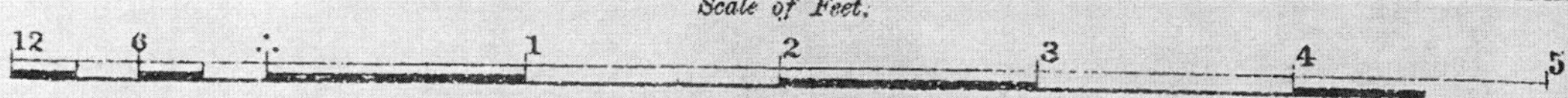

Scale of Feet.

Photo., S. I. O., Calcutta.

Photo., S. I. O., Calcutta.

Scale of Feet.

12 6 0 1 2 3 4 5 6

Photo. S. I. O., Calcutta.

Scale of Feet.

12 6 0 1 2 3 4 5

Photo. S. I. O., Calcutta.

Photo. S. I. O., Calcutta.

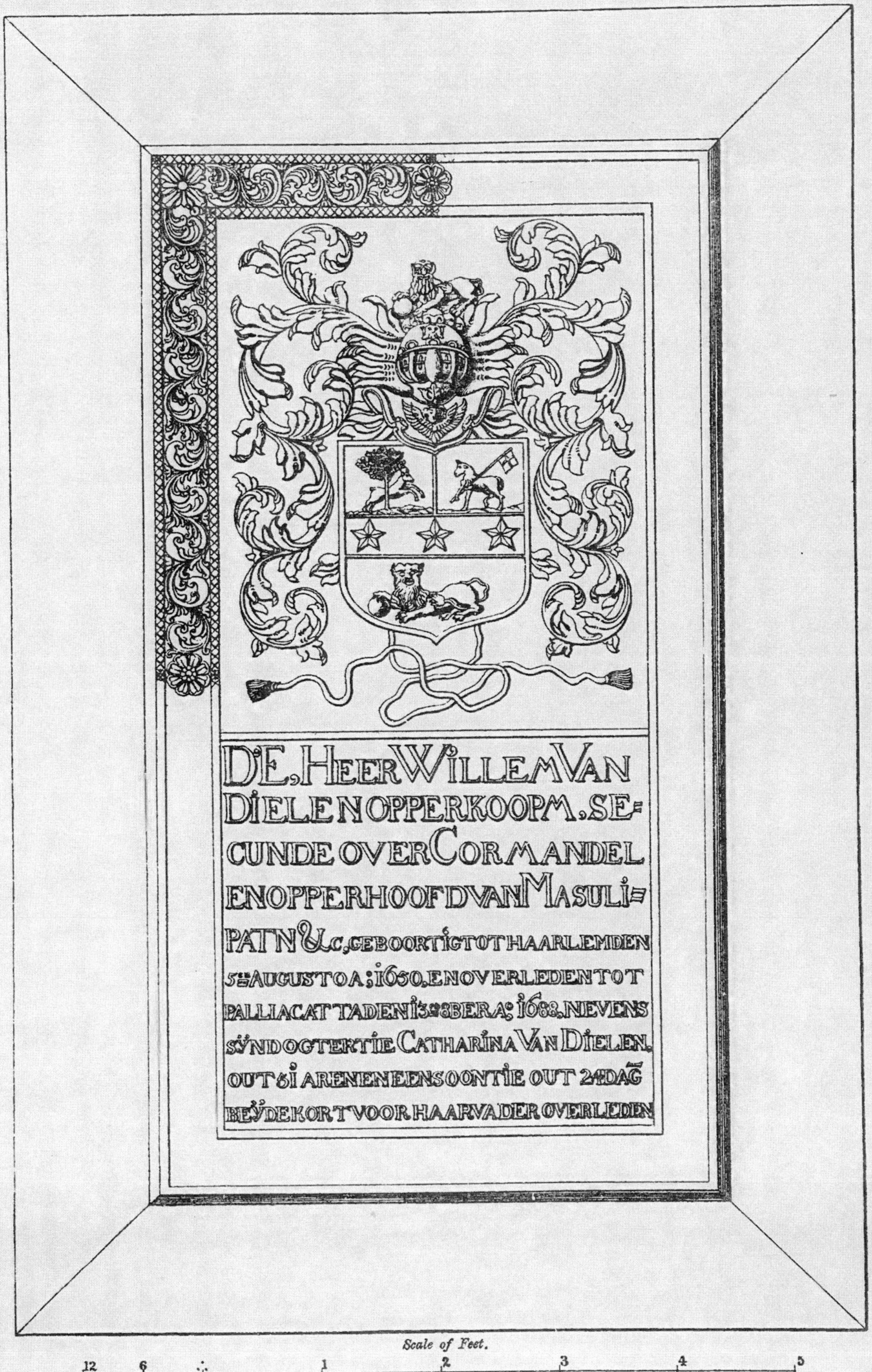

Photo., S. I. O., Calcutta

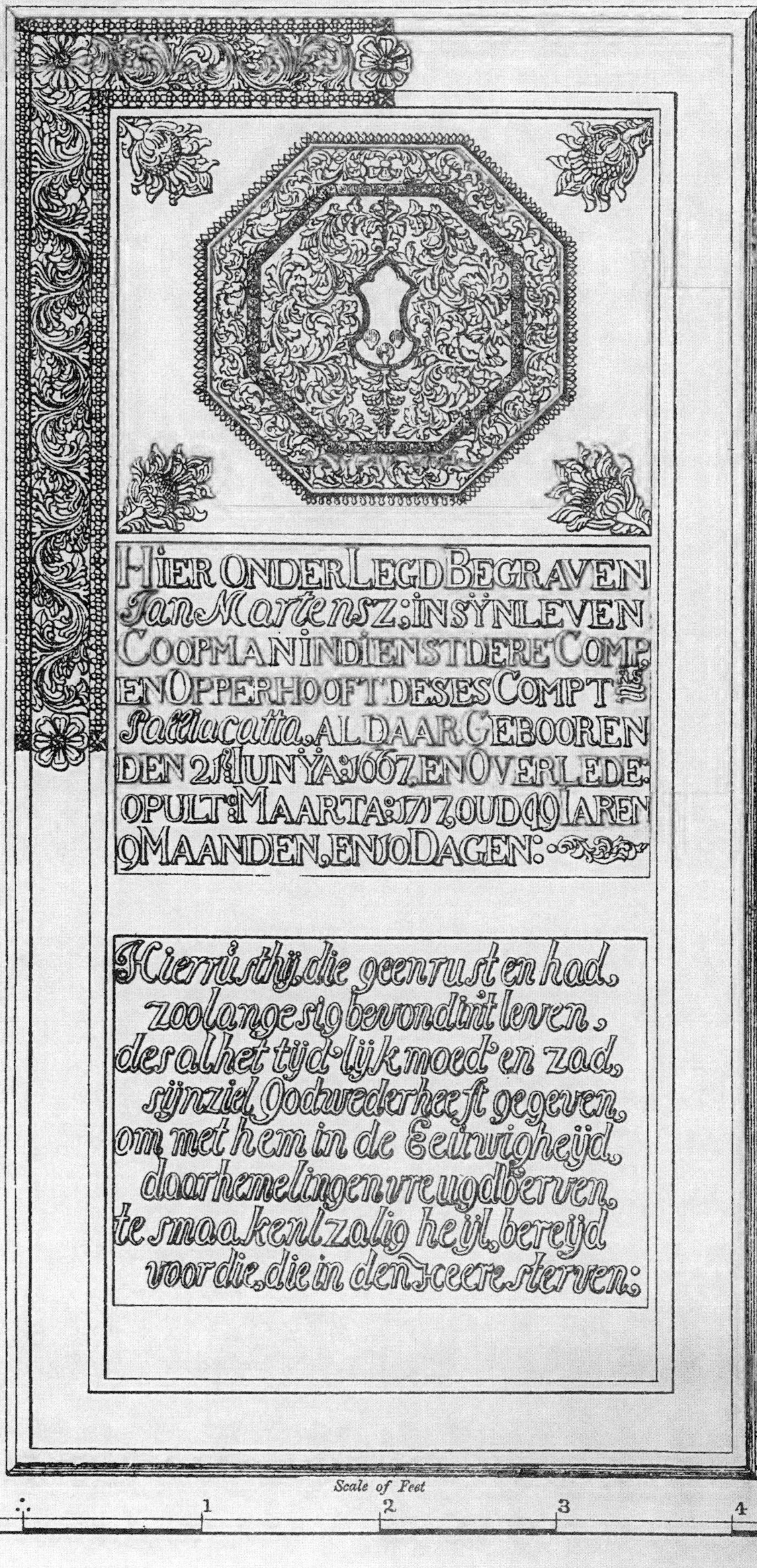

Scale of Feet

12 6 0 1 2 3 4 5

Photo., S. I. O., Calcutta

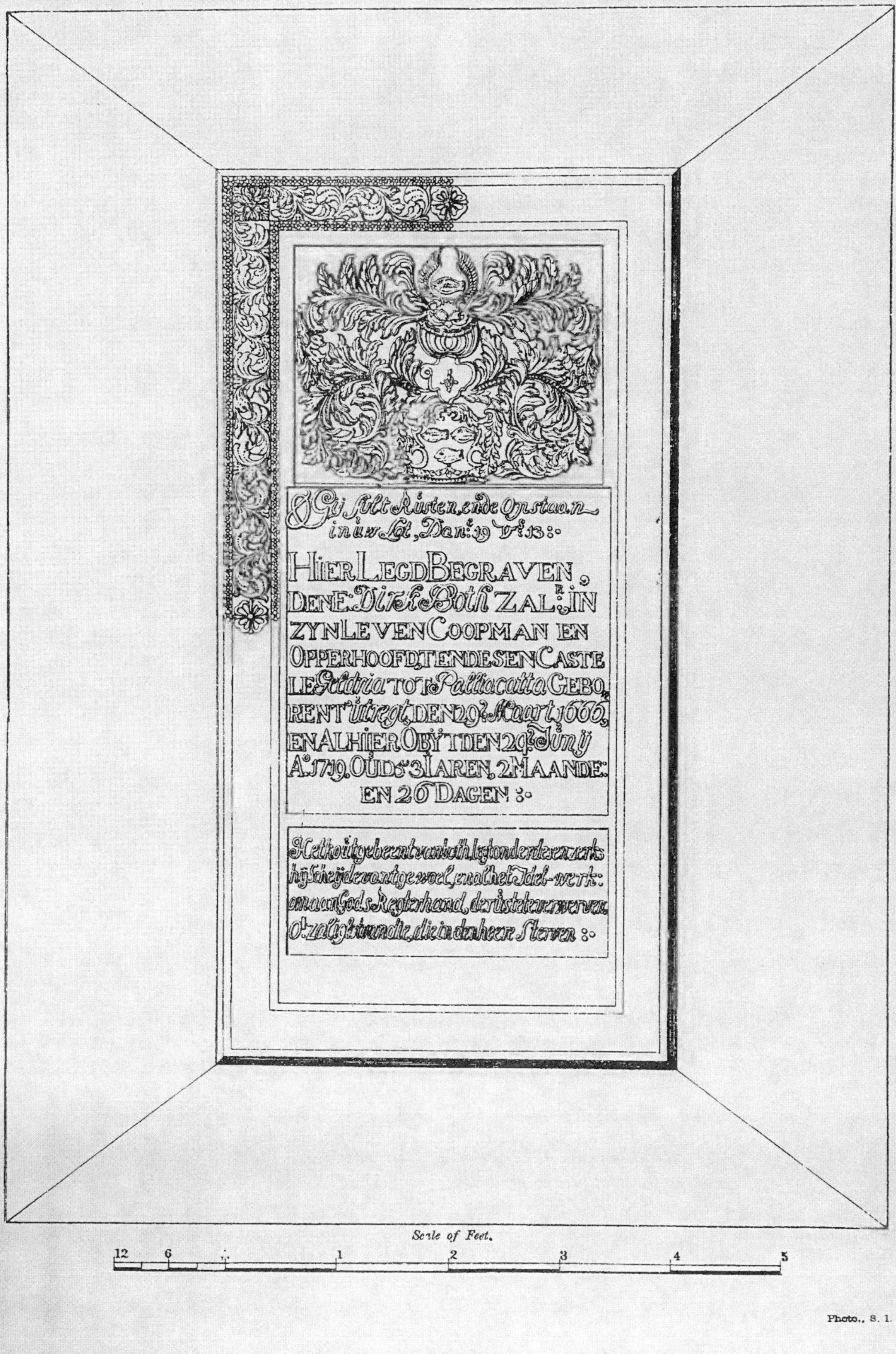

Scale of Feet.

Photo., S. I. O., Calcutta.

Scale of Feet.

12 6 0 1 2 3 4 5

Photo. S. I. O., Calcutta.

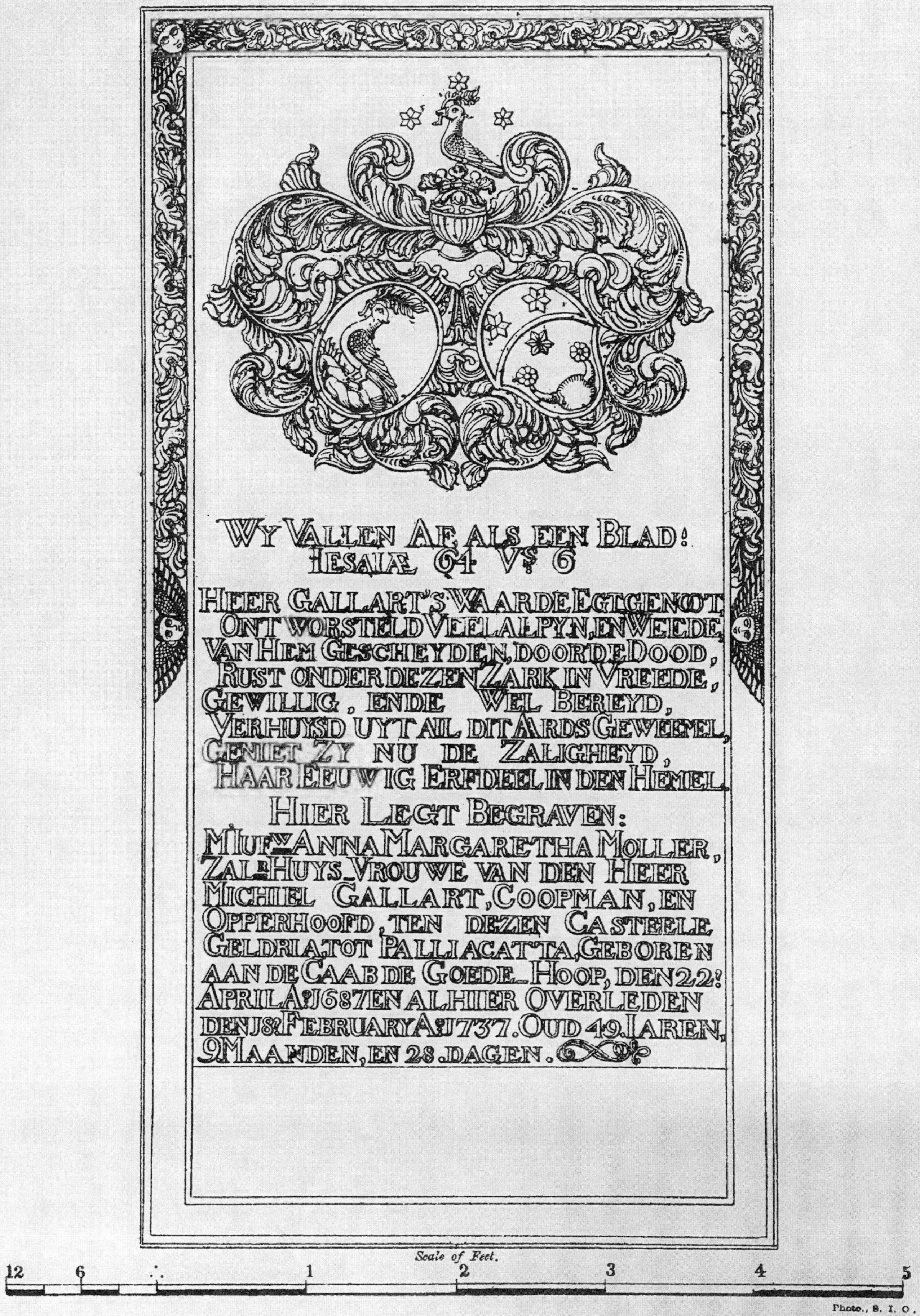

Photo., S. I. O., Calcutta

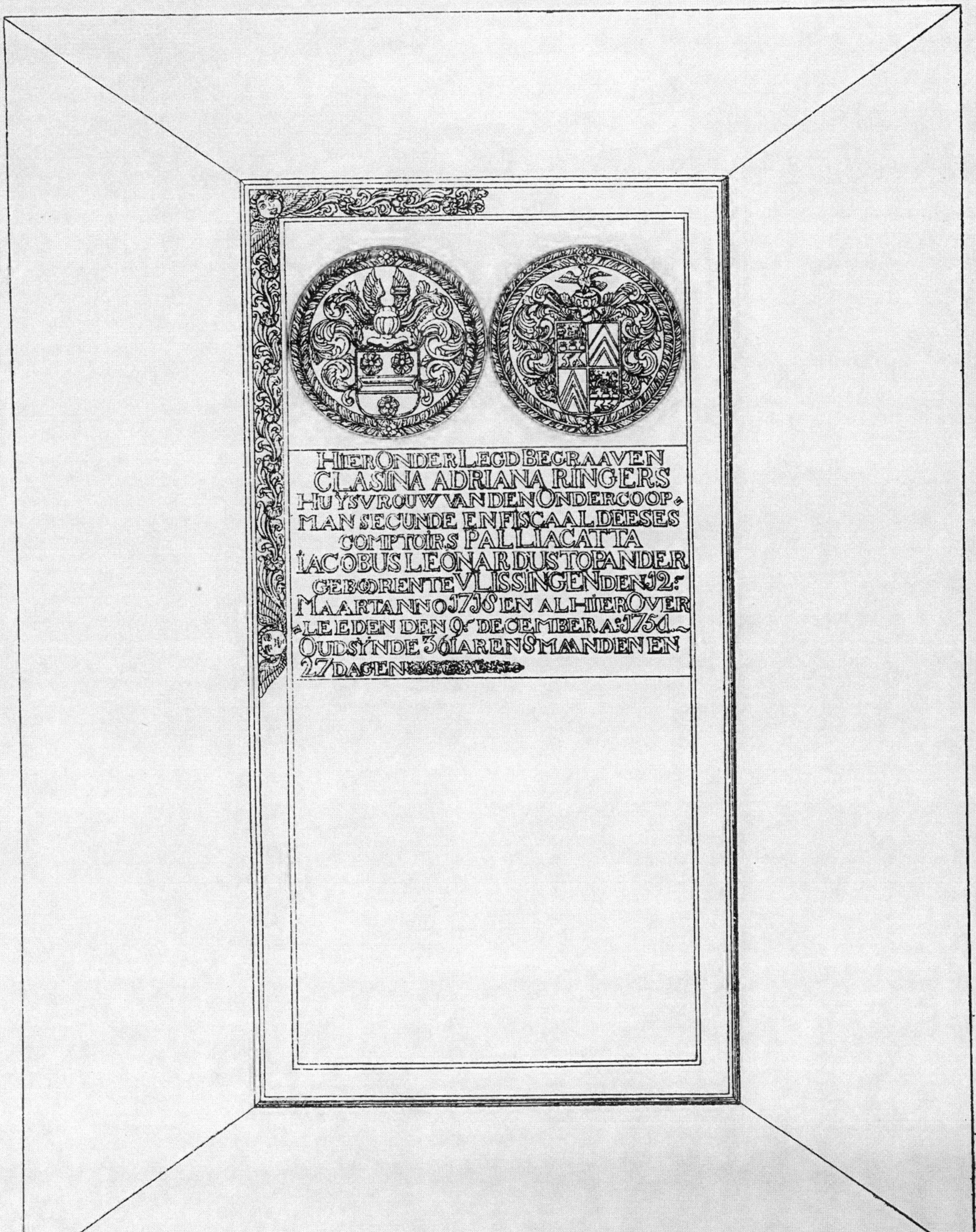

Scale of Feet.

12 6 0 1 2 3 4 5

Photo. S. I. O., Calcutta.

Scale of Feet.

12 6 0 1 2 3 4 5 6 7 8 9 10 11 12 13

Photo. S. I. O., Calcutta.

Scale of Feet. S.N.A

12 6 ∴ 1 2 3 4 5

Photo. S. I. O., Calcutta.

Scale ⅙th of Original. Photo., S. I. O., Calcutta.

Fig. 5.

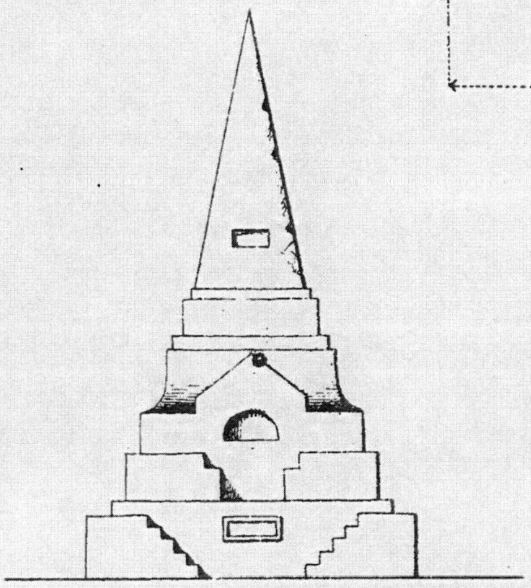

Fig. 1.

Fig. 2.

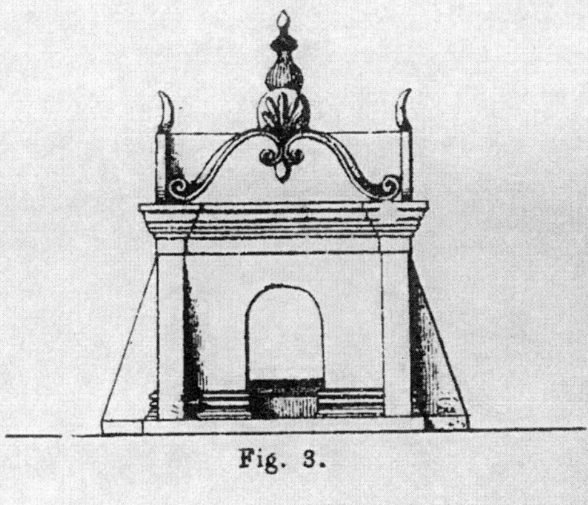

Fig. 3.

No Scale.

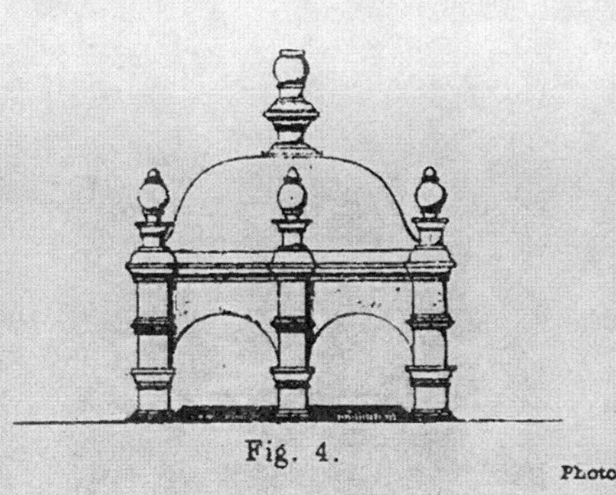

Fig. 4.

Photo. S. I. O., Calcutta.

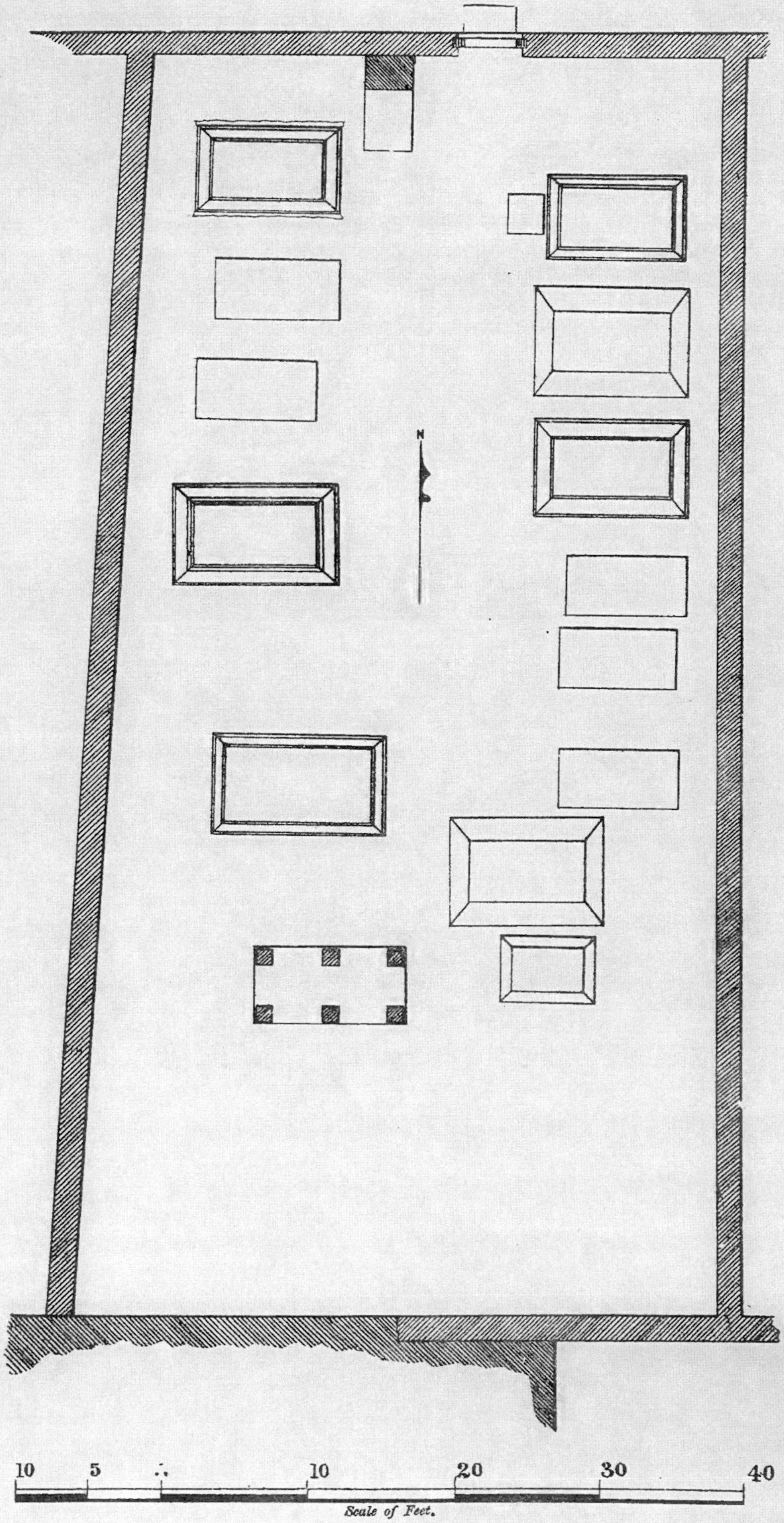

Photo., S. I. O., Calcutta.

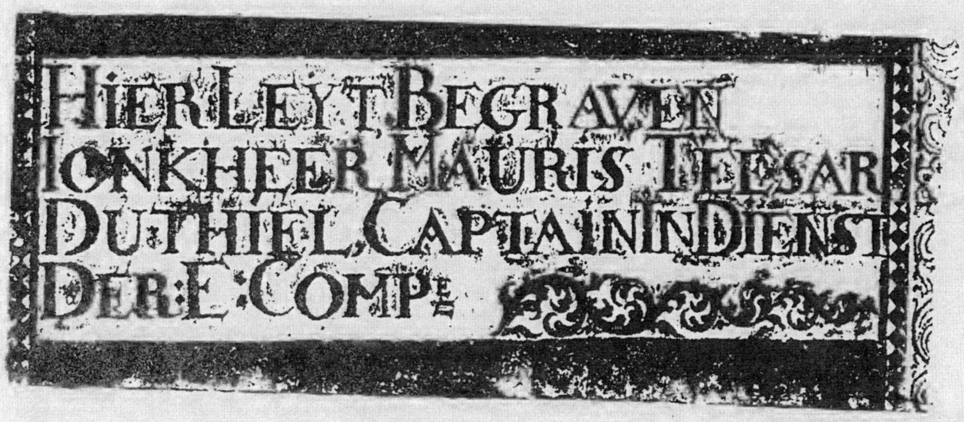

Scale $\frac{1}{8}$th of Original.

Photo., S. I. O., Calcutta.

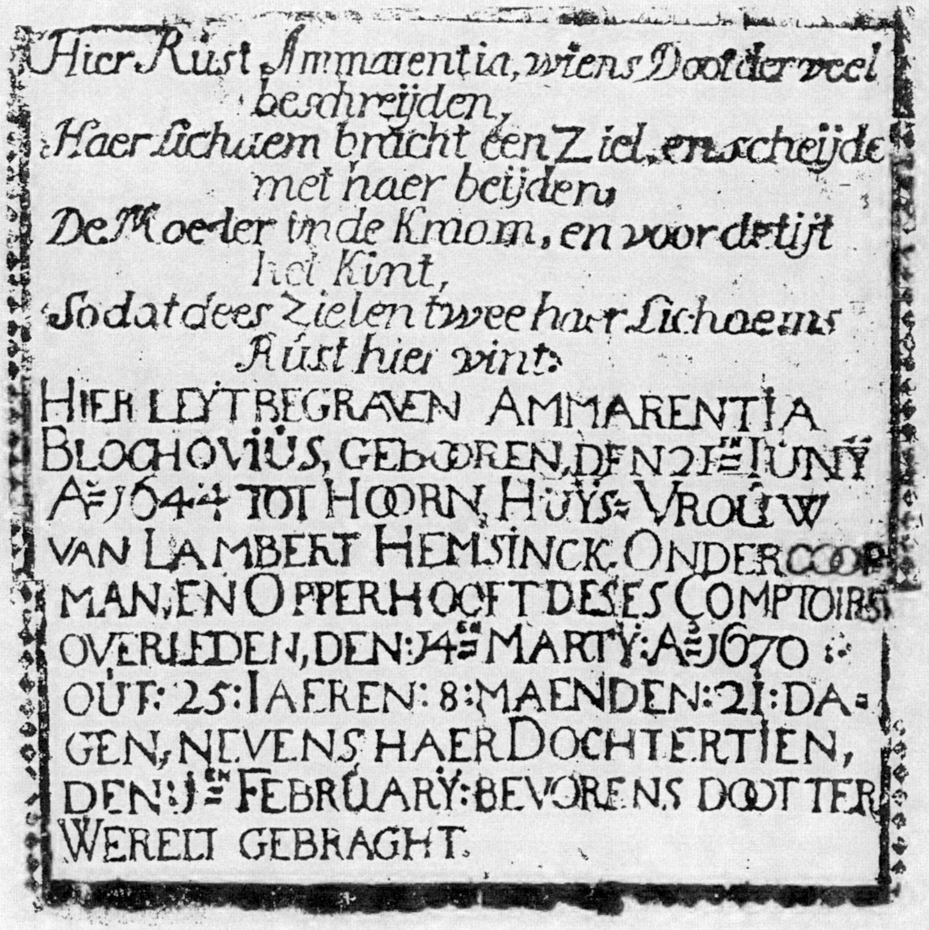
Hier Rúst Ammarentia, wiens Doot der veel
beschreijden,
Haer Lichaem bracht een Ziel, en scheijde
met haer beijden,
De Moeder in de Kraam, en voor de tijt
het Kint,
Sodat dees Zielen twee haer Lichaems
Rúst hier vint:
HIER LEYT BEGRAVEN AMMARENTIA
BLOCHOVIÚS, GEBOOREN DEN 21e IUNIY
Ao 1644 TOT HOORN, HUYS-VROUW
VAN LAMBERT HEMSINCK, ONDERCOOP
MAN, EN OPPERHOOFT DESES COMPTOIRS
OVERLEDEN, DEN: 14e MARTY: Ao 1670:
OÚT: 25: IAEREN: 8: MAENDEN: 21: DA-
GEN, NEVENS HAER DOCHTERTIEN,
DEN: 1e FEBRUARY: BEVORENS DOOT TER
WERELT GEBRAGHT.

Scale 1/8th of Original.

Photo. S. I. O., Calcutta.

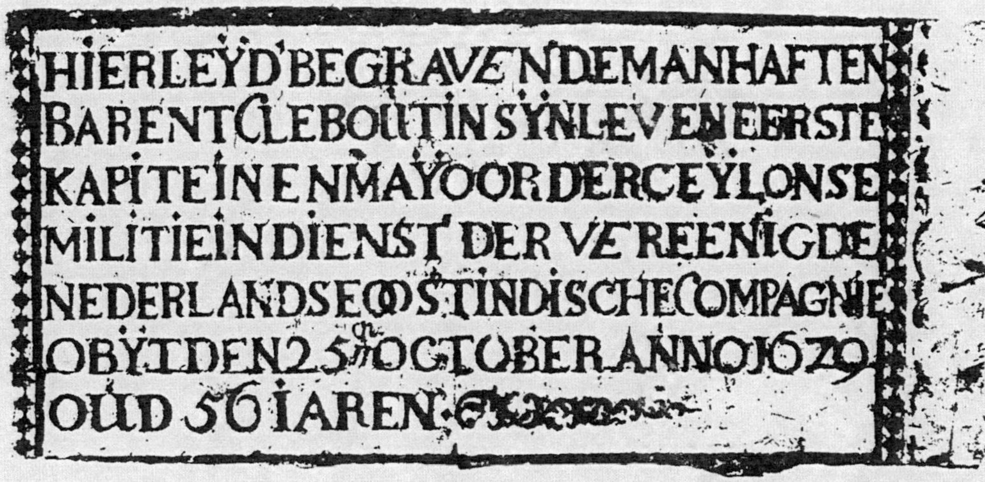

Scale ⅛th of Original.

Photo., S. I. O., Calcutta

Photo. S. I. O., Calcutta.

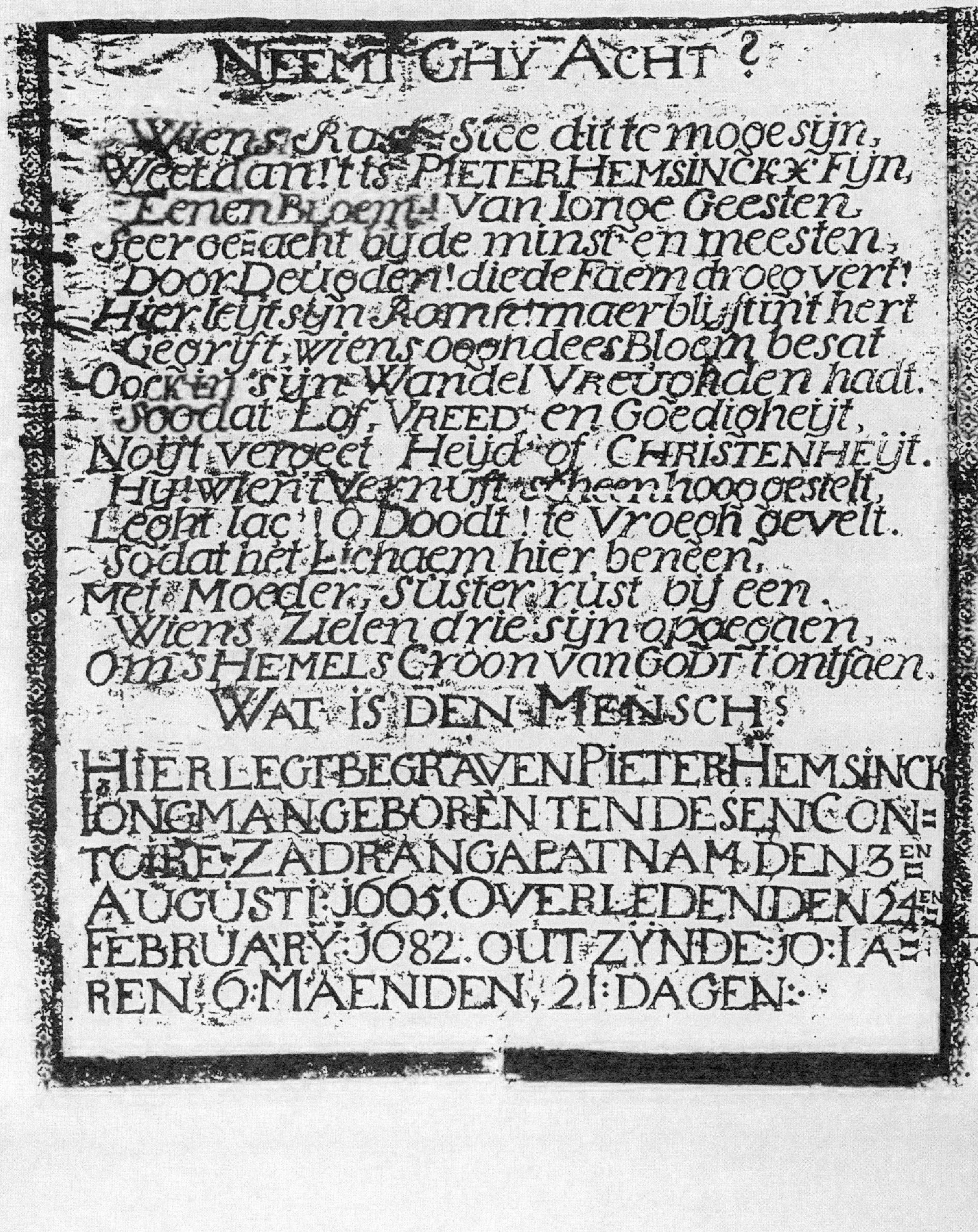

NEEMT GHY ACHT ?

Wiens Rust Stee ditt te moge syn,
Weet dan! t'is PIETER HEMSINCKX Fyn,
Eenen Bloem! Van Ionge Geesten
Seer geacht by de minst en meesten,
Door Deugden! die de Faem droeg vert!
Hier leyt syn Romp; maer blyft in't hert
Gegrift, wiens oogen dees Bloem besat
Oock in syn Wandel Vreughden hadt.
Soodat Lof, VREED en Goedigheyt,
Nooyt vergeet Heyd of CHRISTENHEYT.
Hy! wien't Vernuft scheen hoog gestelt,
Leght lac! O Doodt! te Vroegh gevelt.
Sodat het Lichaem hier beneen,
Met Moeder, Suster rust by een.
Wiens Zielen drie syn opgegaen,
Om 's HEMELS Croon van GODT t'ontfaen.

WAT IS DEN MENSCH?

HIER LEGT BEGRAVEN PIETER HEMSINCK
IONGMAN GEBOREN TEN DESEN CON:
TOIRE ZADRANGAPATNAM DEN 3EN
AUGUSTI: 1665. OVERLEDEN DEN 24EN
FEBRUARY 1682. OUT ZYNDE 16 IA:
REN, 6 MAENDEN, 21 DAGEN.

Scale 1/8th of Original.

Photo. S. I. O., Calcutta.

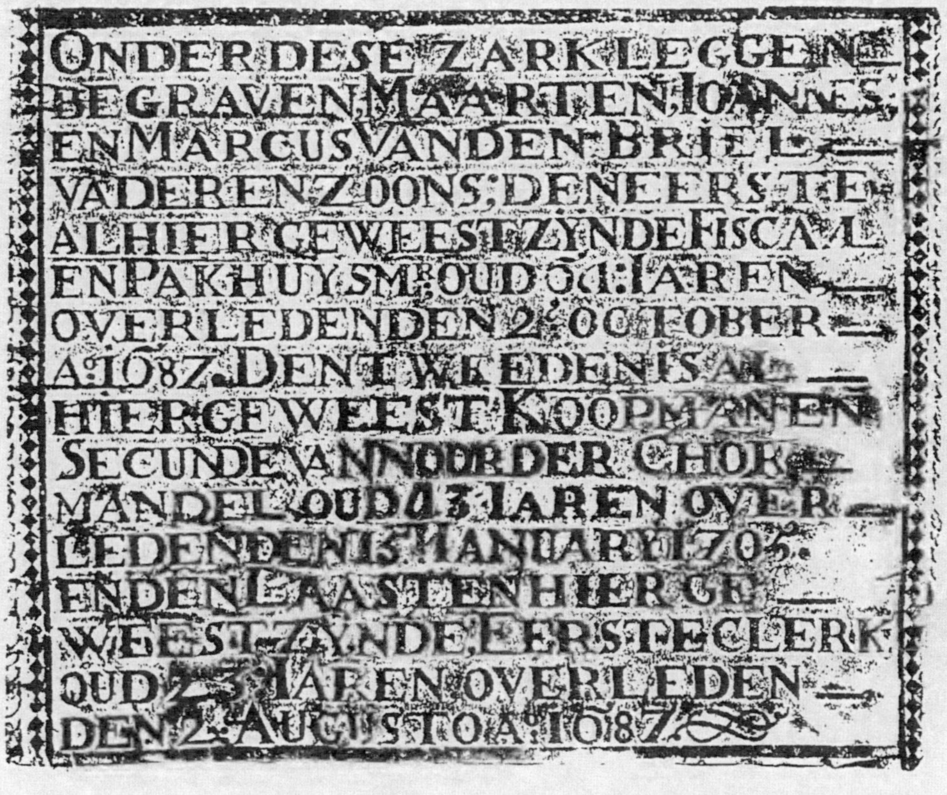

Scale ⅛th of Original.

Photo., S. I. O., Calcutta.

Scale ⅛th of Original.

Photo., S. I. O., Calcutta.

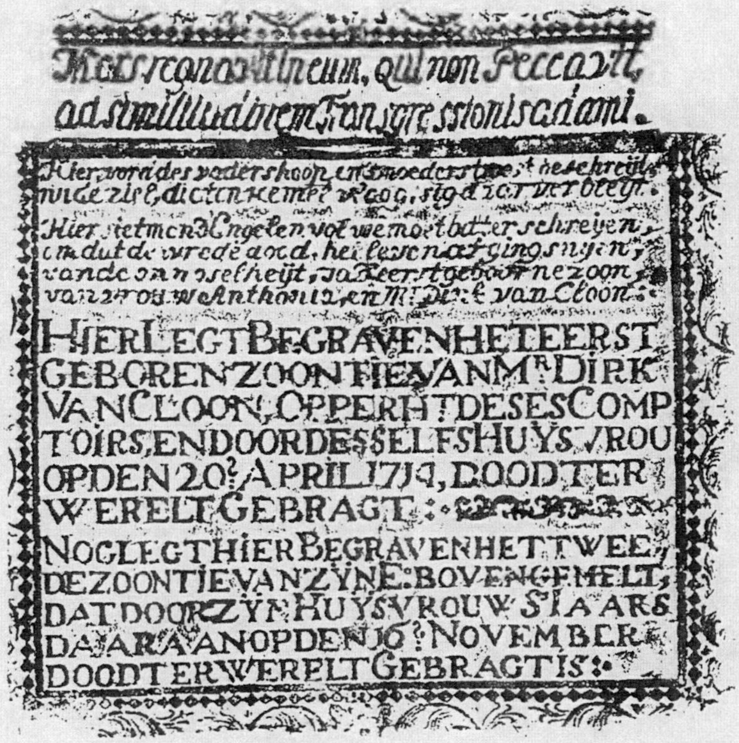

Scale ⅛th of Original.

Photo. S. I. O., Calcutta

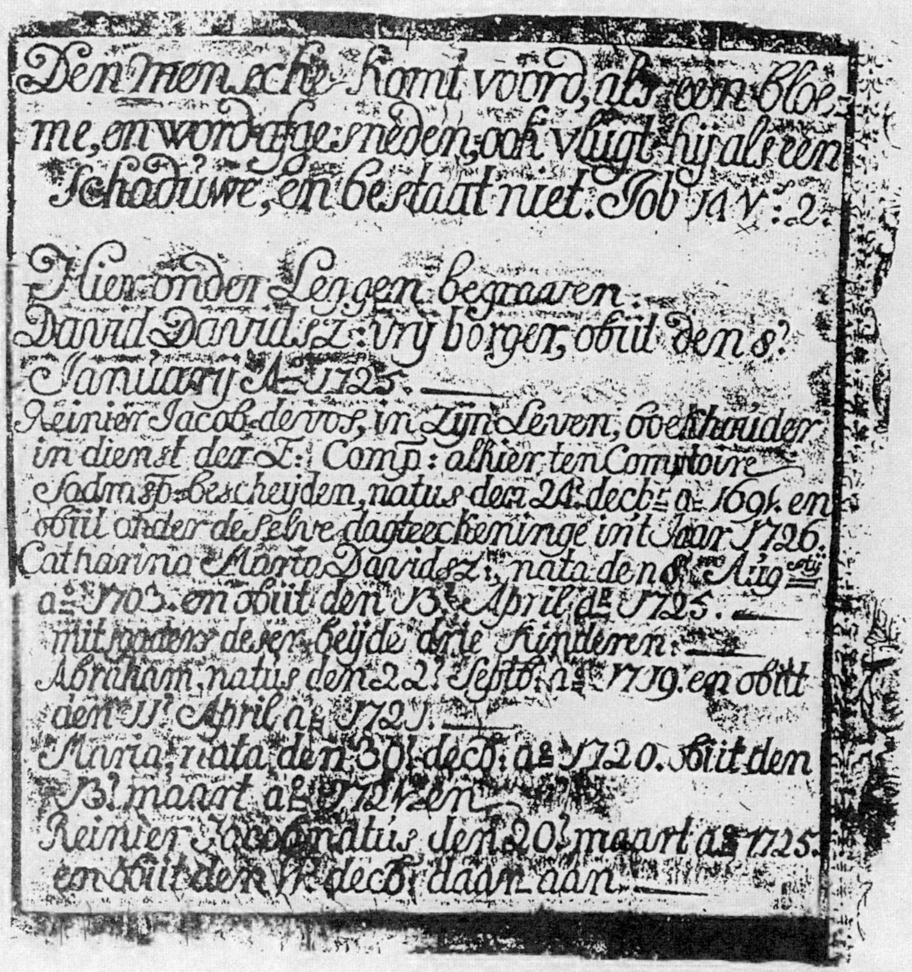

Scale ⅛th of Original.

Photo., S. I. O., Calcutta.

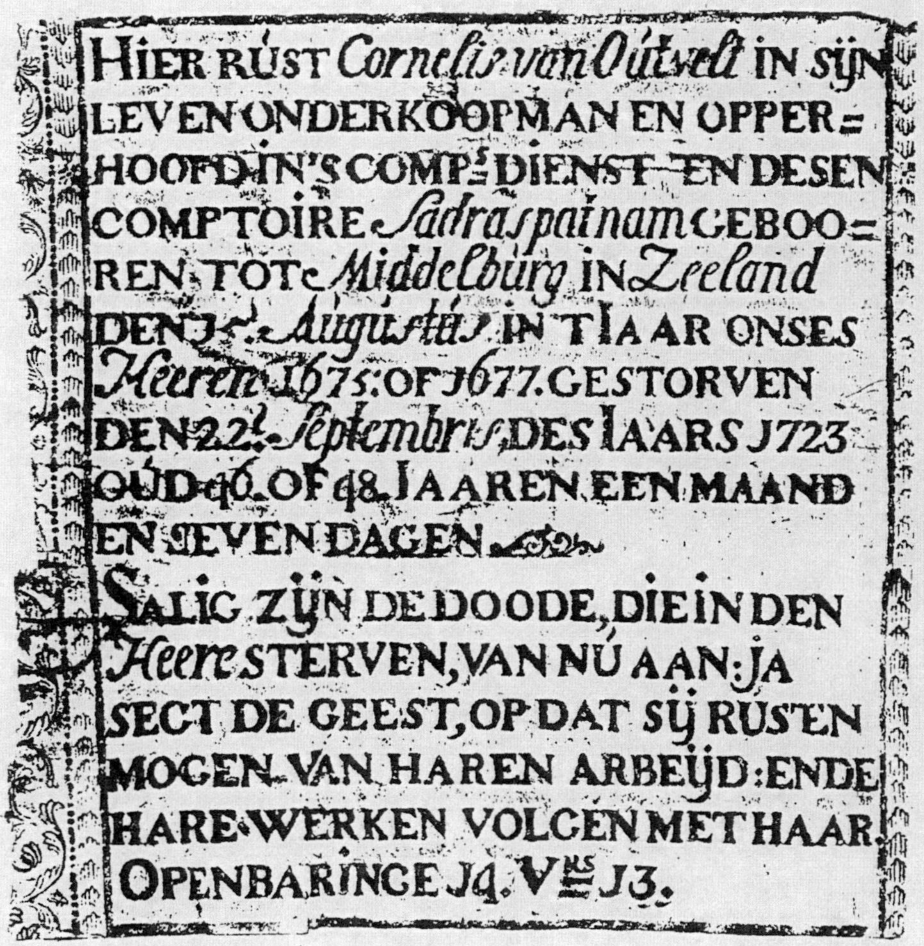

HIER RUST *Cornelis van Outvelt* IN SYN
LEVEN ONDERKOOPMAN EN OPPER=
HOOFD IN 'S COMP^s DIENST EN DESEN
COMPTOIRE *Sadraspatnam* GEBOO=
REN TOT *Middelburg* IN *Zeeland*
DEN 15 *Augustus* IN T IAAR ONSES
Heeren 1675: OF 1677. GESTORVEN
DEN 22^e *Septembris* DES IAARS 1723
OUD 46 OF 48 IAAREN EEN MAAND
EN SEVEN DAGEN
SALIG ZYN DE DOODE, DIE IN DEN
Heere STERVEN, VAN NU AAN: JA
SECT DE GEEST, OP DAT SY RUSTEN
MOGEN VAN HAREN ARBEYD: ENDE
HARE WERKEN VOLGEN MET HAAR.
OPENBARINGE 14. V^ers 13.

Scale ⅛th of Original.

Photo. S. I. O., Calcutta.

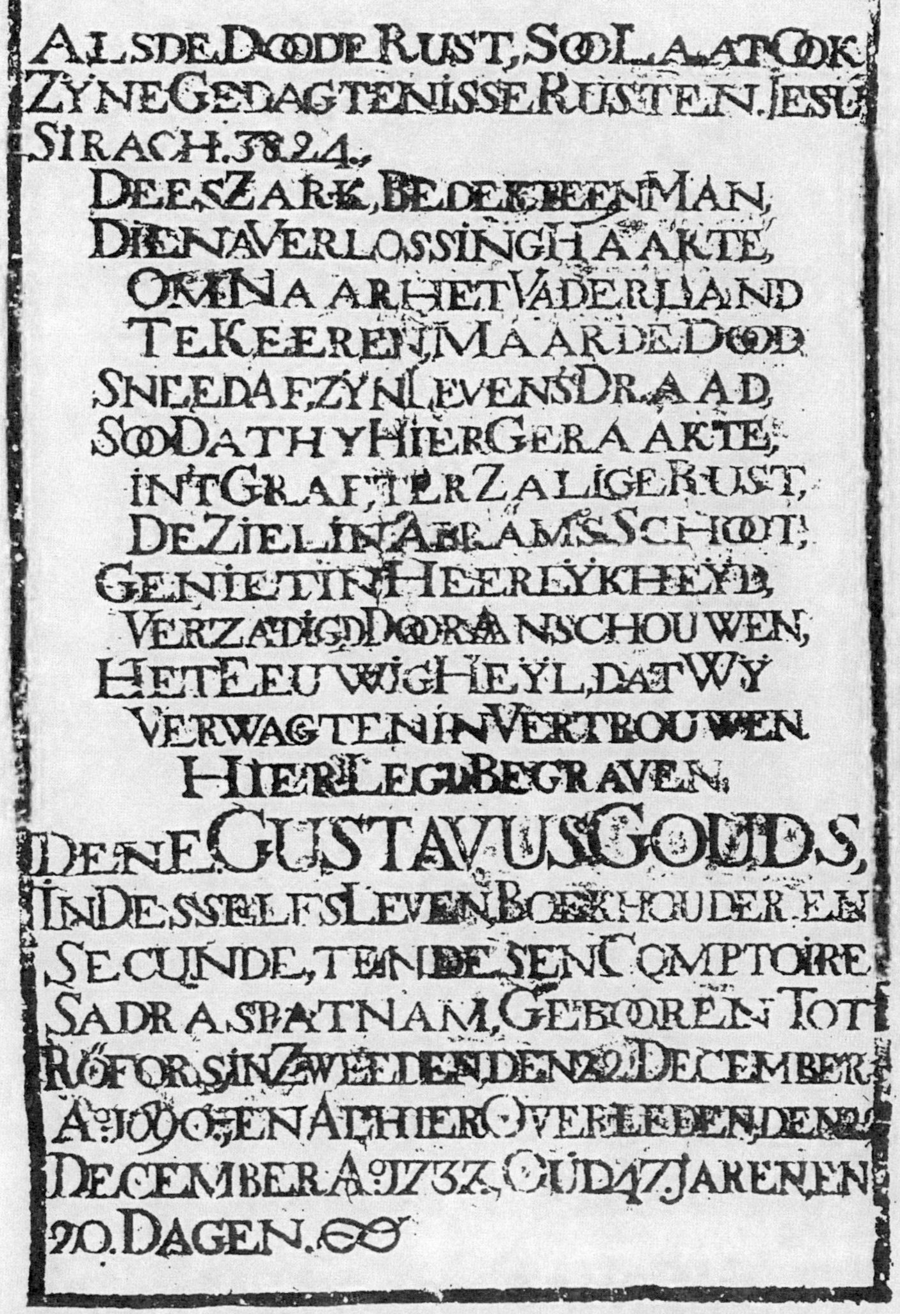
ALS DE DOODE RUST, SOO LAAT OOK
ZYNE GEDAGTENISSE RUSTEN. JESU
SIRACH. 38. 24.
DEES ZARK BEDEKT EEN MAN,
DIE NA VERLOSSING HAAKTE,
OM NAAR HET VADERLAND
TE KEEREN, MAAR DE DOOD
SNEED AF ZYN LEVENS DRAAD,
SOO DAT HY HIER GERAAKTE,
IN'T GRAF, TER ZALIGE RUST,
DE ZIEL IN ABRAMS SCHOOT;
GENIET IN HEERLYKHEYD,
VERZADIGD DOOR ANSCHOUWEN,
HET EEUWIG HEYL, DAT WY
VERWAGTEN IN VERTROUWEN.
HIER LEGD BEGRAVEN,
DEN E. GUSTAVUS GOUDS,
IN DESSELFS LEVEN BOEKHOUDER EN
SECUNDE, TEN DESEN COMPTOIRE
SADRASPATNAM, GEBOOREN TOT
RÖFORS IN ZWEEDEN, DEN 22 DECEMBER
Aº. 1690, EN ALHIER OVERLEEDEN, DEN 2
DECEMBER Aº. 1737, OUD 47 JAREN EN
20. DAGEN.

Scale ⅛th of Original.

Photo., S. I. O., Calcutta.

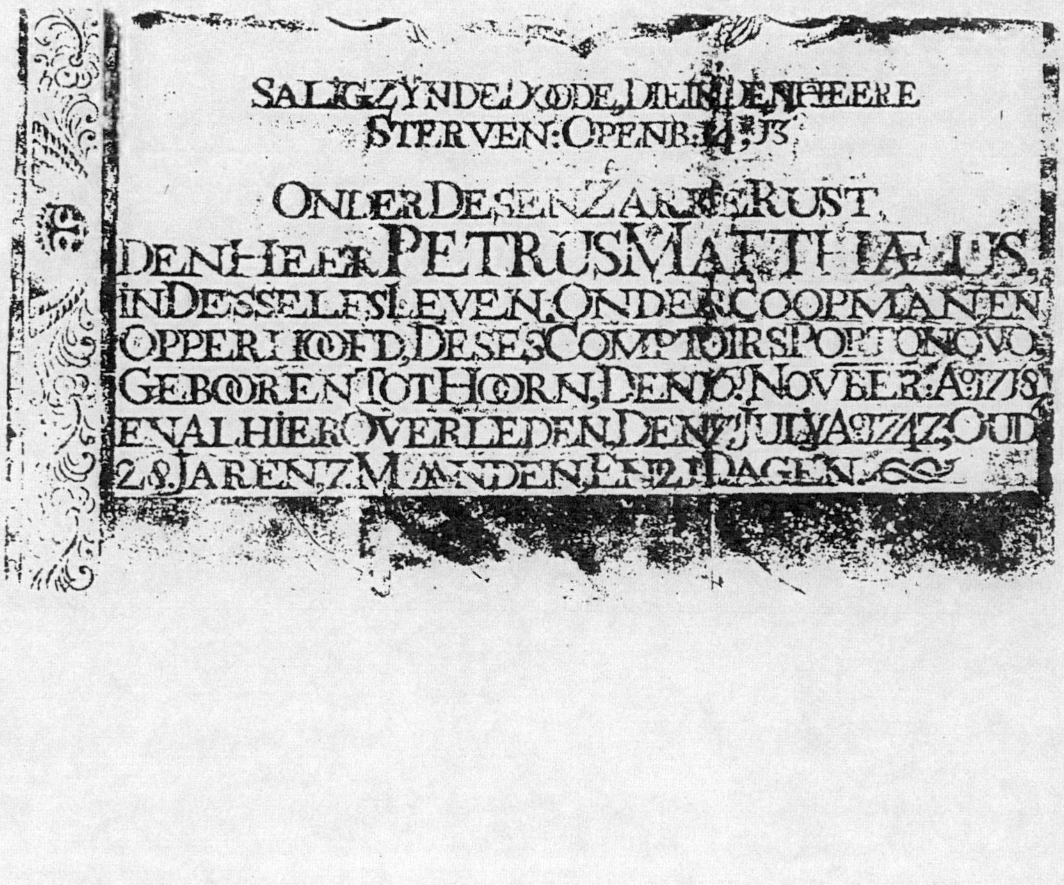

Scale ⅛th of Original.

Photo. S. I. O., Calcutta.

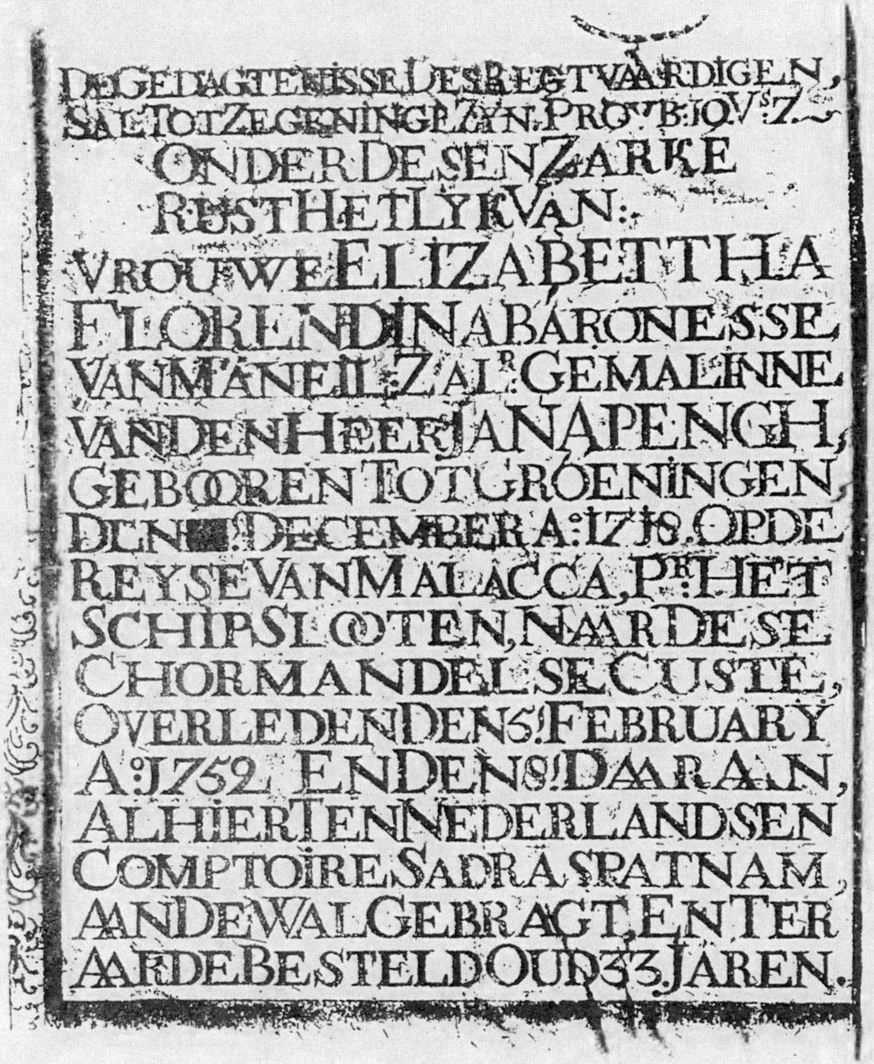

Scale ⅛th of Original.

Photo., S. I. O., Calcutta.

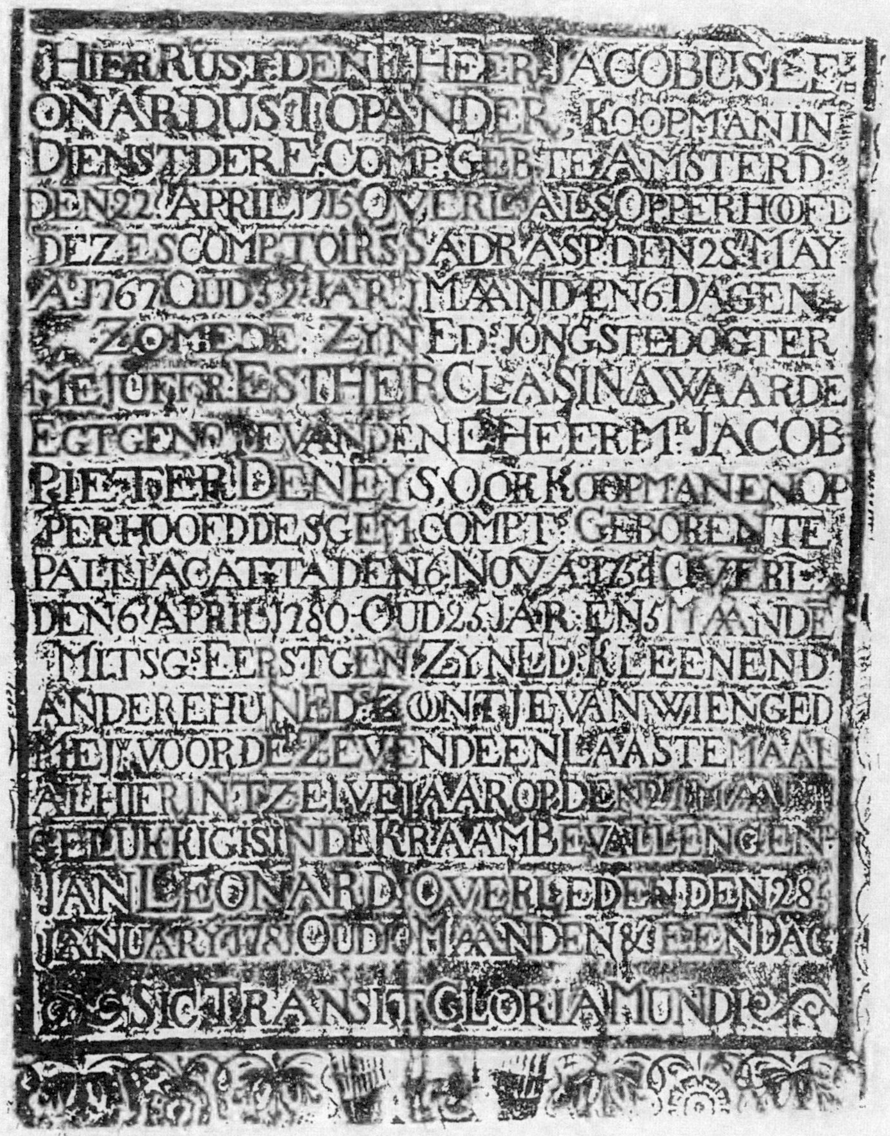

Scale ⅛th of Original.

Photo. S. I. O., Calcutta.

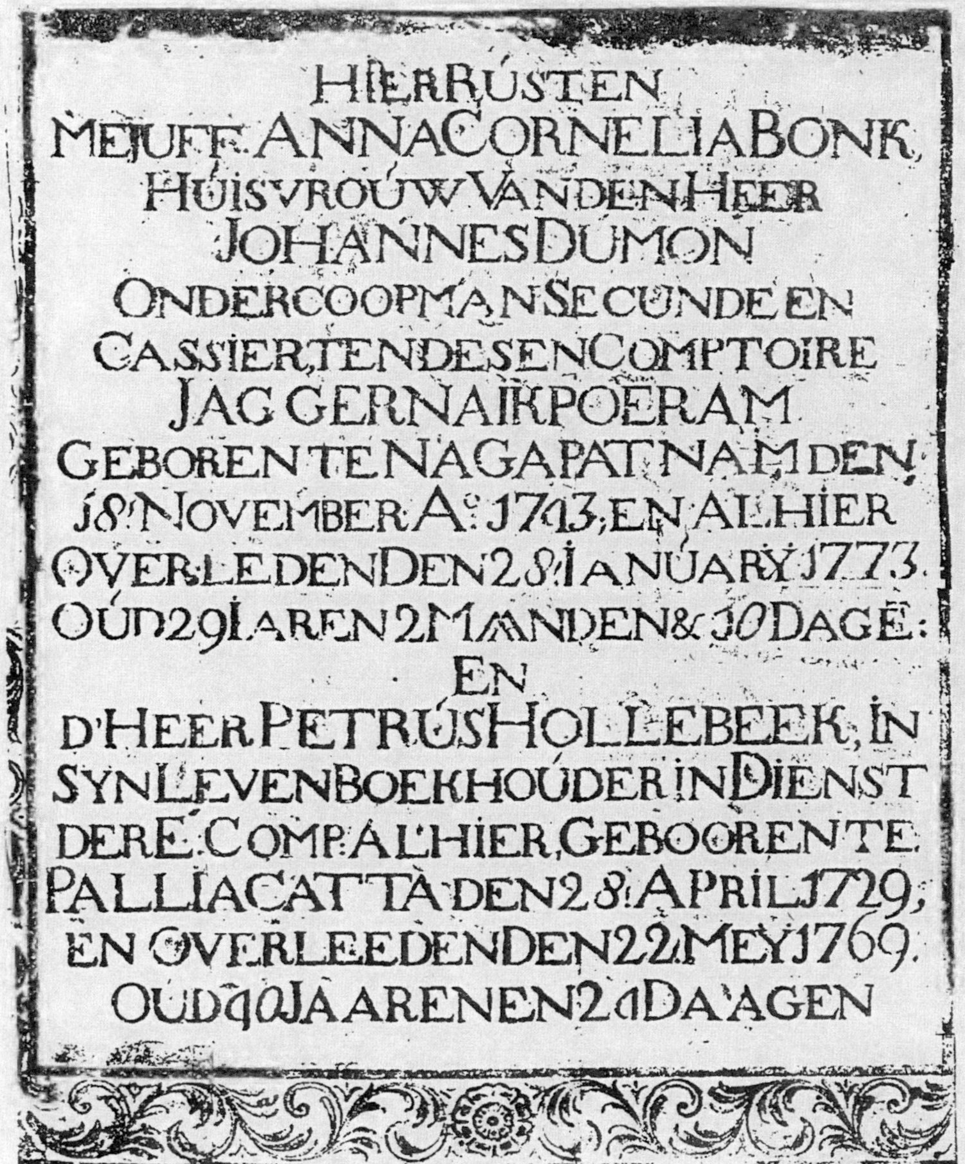

Scale 1/8th of Original.

Photo., S. I. O., Calcutta.

Scale 1/8th of Original.

Photo. S. I. O., Calcutta.

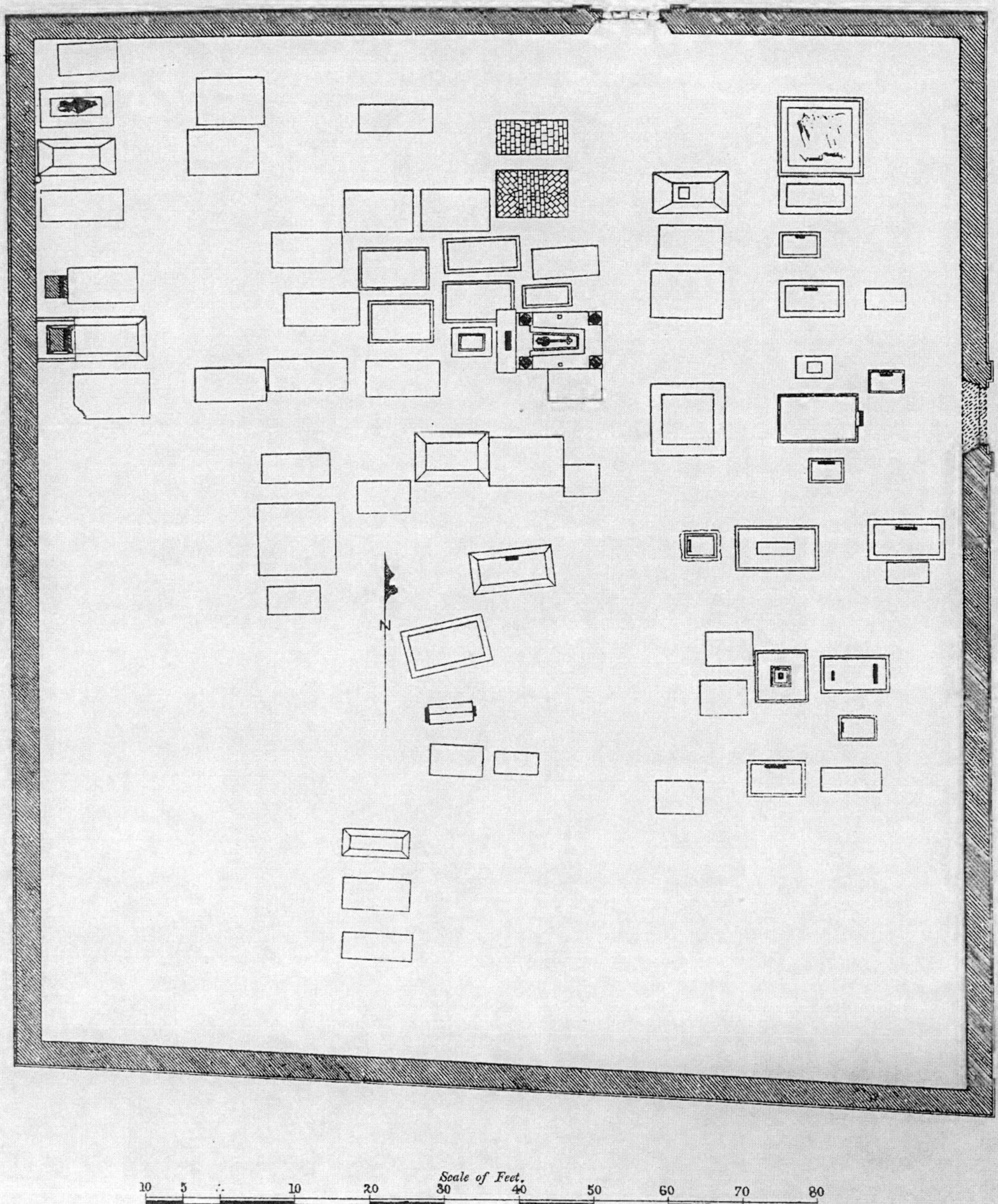

Photo., S. I. O., Calcutta.

Scale of Feet.

Photo. S. I. O., Calcutta.

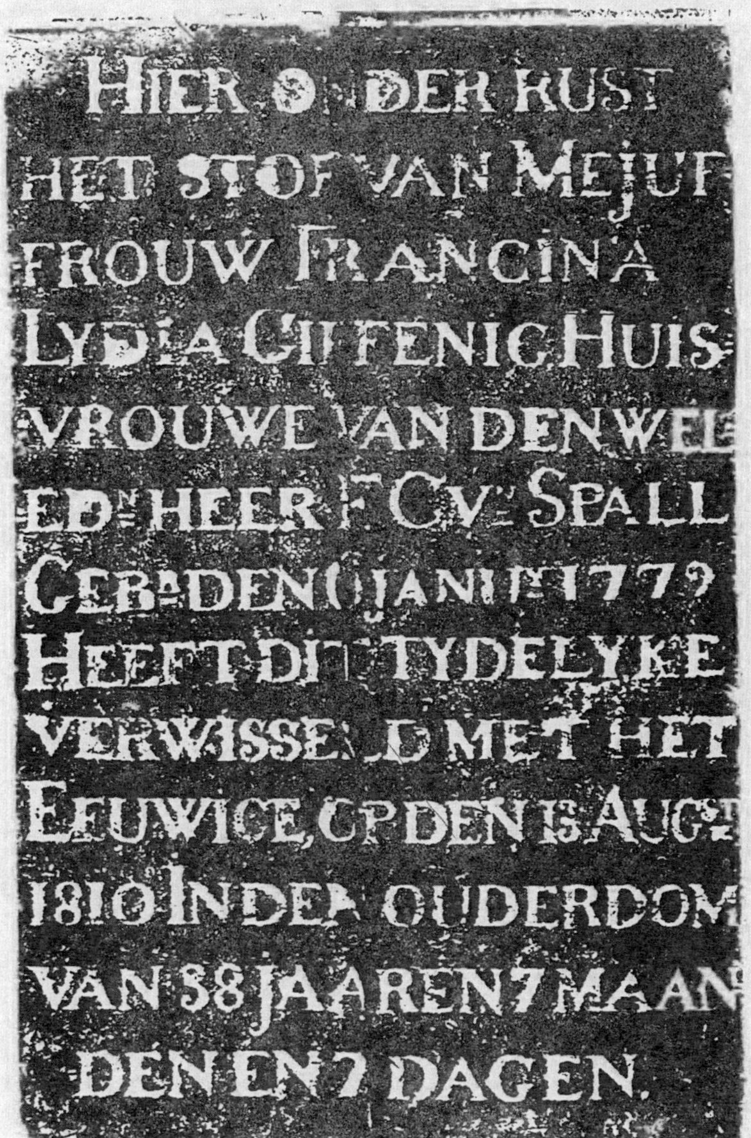

Scale ⅛th of Original.

Photo., S. I. O., Calcutta.

Scale 1/8th of Original.

Photo. S. I. O., Calcutta.

Scale of Feet

Photo. S. I. O., Calcutta.

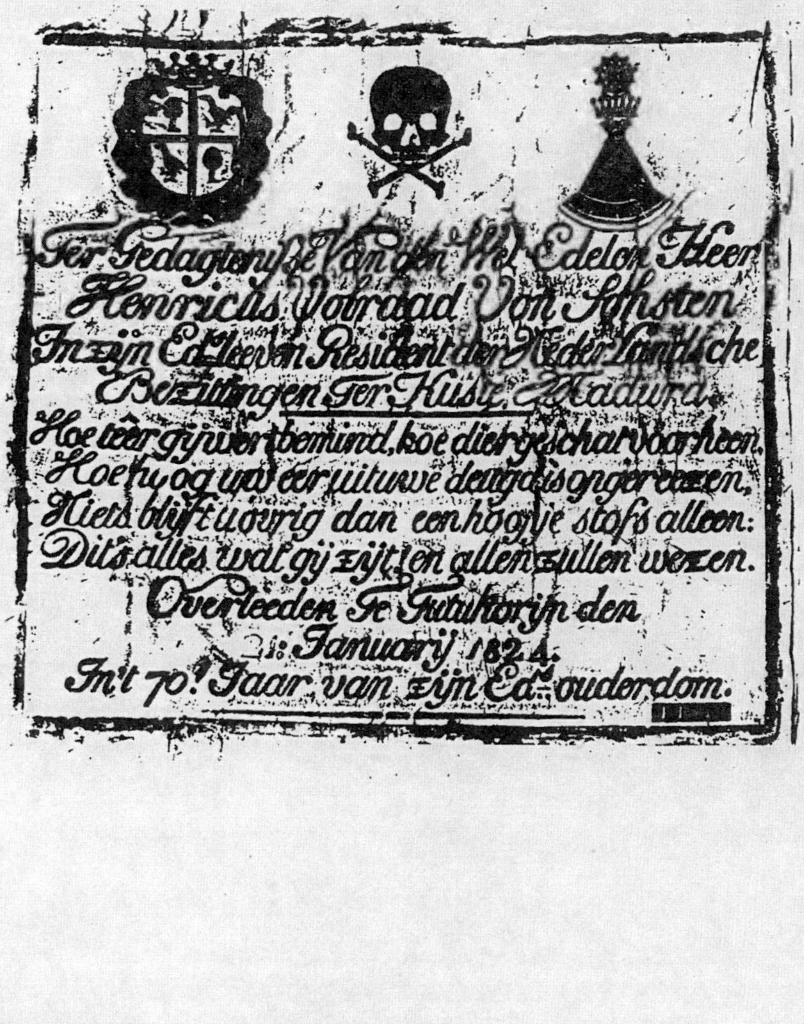

Ter Gedagtenisse Van den Wel Edelen Heer
Henricus Volraad Von Sohsten
In zijn Ed: leeven Resident der Neder Landsche
Bezittingen Ter Kust Madura.
Hoe teer gij wiert bemind, hoe diep geschat voorheen,
Hoe hoog uw eer uit uwe deugd is opgerezen,
Niets blijft u overig dan een hoopje stofs alleen:
Dit's alles wat gij zijt, en allen zullen wezen.
Overleeden Te Tuutkorijn den
21: Januarij 1824.
In't 70! Jaar van zijn Ed: ouderdom.

Scale 1/8th of Original.

Photo., S. I. O., Calcutta

INDO-DUTCH COINAGE

PLATE LXIII.

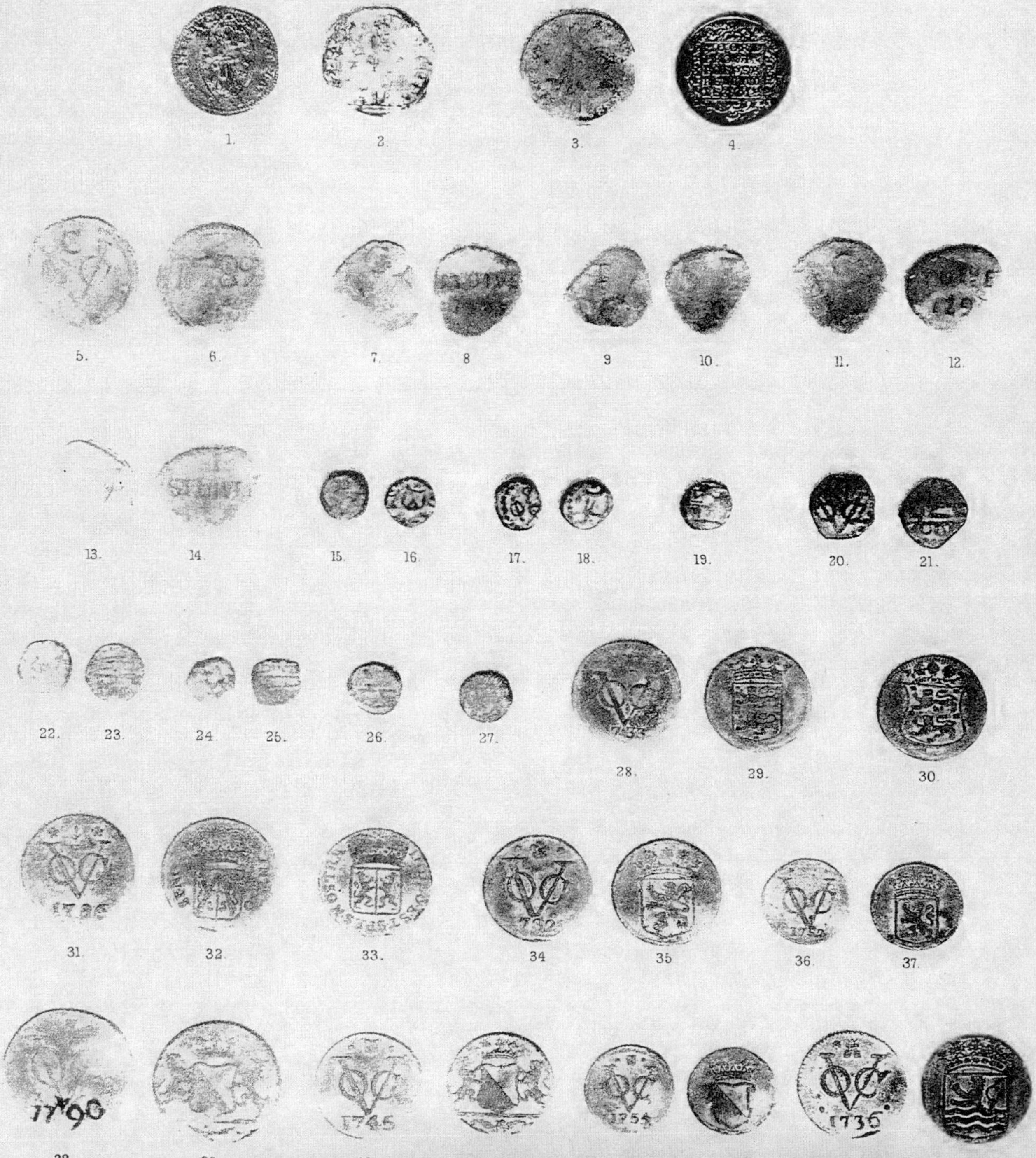

Scale $\frac{17}{20}$ths of Originals.

Note. Figs 1 to 4, Gold (2 and 3 are plaster casts) 5 to 27, Indian copper (5 to 14, are plaster casts) 28 to 45, Indo-European copper.

Photo etching.

Survey of India Offices, Calcutta, August 1897.